LAP QUILTING

HOW TO MAKE BEAUTIFUL QUILTED PROJECTS–LARGE & SMALL

MURIEL BRECKENRIDGE

Sterling Publishing Co., Inc.   New York
Distributed in the U.K. by Blandford Press

Diagrams by Al Breckenridge
Photographs by Al Breckenridge and
Robin Brass

*This book is affectionately dedicated to my father, Floyd
Vannest, who has passed along to me some of his craftsmanship
and his love for creating beautiful things.*

Acknowledgements

I would like to thank Robin Brass, Managing Editor of Canadian
Trade Books for McGraw-Hill Ryerson Limited for his constant
enthusiasm and assistance, especially in aiding with the photography.
I also wish to thank my husband, Al, for the many long hours he
spent in preparing the graphics as well as photographing the articles
for the book. Without his support and work the book would not have
been possible.
M.E.B.

Library of Congress Cataloging in Publication Data
Breckenridge, Muriel
  Lap quilting.
  Includes index.
  1. Quilting. I. Breckenridge, Al. II. Title.
TT835.B69 1981   746.46   81-50545
ISBN 0-8069-5446-9
ISBN 0-8069-5447-7 (lib. bdg.)

ISBN 0-8069-7522-9 (paper)

Published in 1981 by Sterling Publishing Co., Inc.
Two Park Avenue, New York, N.Y. 10016
Distributed in the United Kingdom by Blandford Press
Link House, West Street, Poole, Dorset BH15 1LL, England
First published in Canada by McGraw-Hill Ryerson
© 1980 by Muriel Breckenridge
Manufactured in the United States of America
All rights reserved

Contents

Introduction

When I was young my mother told me that she would never teach me how to quilt for if I did not learn, then I would never have to do it. Quilting meant work for my mother, for as a young girl in her own home she had spent many long winter evenings around the quilting frame helping prepare quilts for family use.

Today, quilting can be great fun as well as a relaxing and creative pastime. With the method of lap quilting which I use in this book, you do not need to worry about a large space in your home to set up quilt frames, since lap quilting is done on a small frame in your lap and smaller articles are quilted on a flat lap board. Quilting today is not reserved for quilts as it was for my mother, but can be used in as many ways as the imagination will allow.

I have written this book with two purposes in mind. One is to provide instruction for new quilters in the art of lap quilting and the second is to introduce an alternative technique to the experienced quilter who may find this method more convenient, especially if living in small quarters.

Lap quilting is known by various names but I often find that it is described as a method of quilting without the use of a frame. After the quilt blocks are sewn together and basted to the batting and lining, it is then either quilted in the lap without a frame, or a quilting hoop is used, working outwards from the centre of the quilt.

This is not the method of lap quilting which I use or have described in this book. My method uses a tapestry frame to which individual blocks or pieces are pinned. The long sides of the frame are turned to adjust the tension on the block and thus the quilting is done on a very smooth and taut surface, preventing unevenness or lumping in the materials or batting. A large quilting hoop, with a screw adjustment on the outside, is used to quilt any areas which cannot be done on the tapestry frame. Smaller pieces, too small for the frame, are done on the hard surface of a lap board.

With this method of lap quilting each block is sewn individually. When the surface of the block is completed, whether it be patchwork, appliqué or a plain block to be ornately quilted, it is placed on a lining or backing material with a piece of quilt batting in between. The layers of the block are then basted together before pinning it onto the tapestry frame for quilting.

Since your quilting is always at hand, you can pick it up quickly and work on it whenever you have a few minutes — while the

4

potatoes are boiling, while you are watching television or having coffee with a friend. Consequently, you can accomplish much in a short time. I know one elderly lady, a student of mine, who carried her quilt blocks in her suitcase and her collapsed frame under her arm when she flew to the West Coast for a visit.

The students in my classes who learn to quilt with this method are extremely enthusiastic about both the ease of quilting and the even and accurate results accomplished. This enthusiasm applies to both new and old quilters for I have students ranging from teen-agers to quilters in their 70's and 80's, many of whom have years of quilting experience on large frames.

The variety of articles which can be made is limited only by your imagination. All quilted articles make beautiful and much-appreciated gifts. Several of my students have made shower and even wedding gifts from quilted articles, sets of place-mats being a favourite.

All the projects which I have described and given directions for in this book I have made myself. Learn to create your own designs and sew whatever you fancy. Happy quilting!

A Thumb-Nail Sketch of the History of Quilting

Through the ages quilting has been both an economic necessity for the poor and a creative art for the more affluent. It is as old as Ancient Egypt where, in Biblical times, Pharaohs wore quilted garments as protection against the sun, and China where the ancient Chinese and Mongolian tribes wore such clothing for warmth in their severely cold climate. Quilted clothing was also worn in India and the Ancient Greeks and Romans used quilts as well as quilted sleeping pads.

The art of quilting was brought to Europe in the 11th century by the Crusaders where it immediately became popular. In the 14th century several severely cold winters forced European people to turn to quilted bed covers as well as clothing, curtains and wall-hangings as a form of protection against the cold walls of draughty castles. Sometimes thick feather or wool comforters were made with a minimum of quilting or by tying the layers together.

Patchwork is the oldest form of quilting. At first a necessity in poor homes where patches were made from old and worn garments and stitched into new clothing and quilts, its decorative value quickly became recognized and middle- and upper-class homes were soon making use of it. In 1540, when Henry VIII married Catharine Howard, he presented her with 23 quilts as one of his wedding gifts. It is said that Mary, Queen of Scots, while imprisoned, spent many long hours piecing together patches for quilts and Queen Elizabeth I wore gowns quilted with gold and silver thread.

Because of their economy, patchwork quilts were indispensable in the early years of colonial America. Quilters took great pride in designing their patterns from the world of nature around them. A housewife's piece bag was a cherished possession and every scrap was put to use, thus accounting for the crazy patchwork quilt's rise to popularity. Women learned, often from friendly Indians, how to make dyes from weeds, lichen, and flowers. When uncarded wool was scarce for interlinings the pioneers used wild birds' feathers, down from geese and even cat-tail down. Since textiles were imported into Canada until the middle of the 19th century and were therefore expensive, home-grown flax and sheep's wool, spun and woven into fabric, were most commonly used. Homespun linen thread was used for sewing and quilting.

Through the ages appliqué has been used for the decoration of religious robes and hangings, in court clothing and banners as well as quilts. Crusading knights used appliquéd motifs on their cloaks and banners as identification for themselves. Because fabric was both scarce and expensive appliqué was not used at first by settlers because they could not afford to place one layer of cloth over another. It became more popular when textiles began to be manufactured in North America. The first cotton mill in Canada was opened in Sherbrooke, Quebec, in 1845.

In the early years a quilting frame was a part of almost every household and long winter evenings were spent in preparing new quilts for the family. Besides these quilts every girl was expected to prepare 12 quilts as part of her dowry. The final bridal quilt was not sewn until after her engagement. In those early days the quilting frame was in constant use. In homes too small to spare space for the large frame a pulley system was used to pull it up to the ceiling when not in use. The advent of the sewing machine, the new woven wool blankets and lack of space to erect large frames caused quilting to decline in popularity but in recent years we are once again discovering the artistic value of quilting. It is now considered to be a fabric art. As in all things, we modernize our methods and quilting virtually done in the lap has helped to solve the problem of space in which to set up large quilting frames.

1 Quilt Materials and Templates

BASIC QUILTING SUPPLY LIST

Needles	*"Quilting" needles, 1 package.*
Thread	*Quilting thread, cotton or polyester thread as you prefer.*
Thimble	*Essential — get a good fit and learn to use it.*
Sandpaper	*1 sheet, medium grade, to glue on templates.*
Glue	*1 glue stick to glue sandpaper.*
Templates or patterns	*Bristol board, stiff cardboard or flat pieces of plastic cut from used containers.*
Pencils	*1 soft lead B, 1 medium-hard lead, 1 white lead for marking dark cottons.*
Scissors	*1 pair for cutting sandpaper and cardboard, 1 sharp pair with blades at least 4" (10 cm) long for cutting fabrics.*
Straight pins	*A plentiful supply.*
Ruler	*6" (15 cm) long*
Art gum	*For removing quilting lines if necessary.*
Quilting frames	*27" (70 cm) tapestry frame. If this size is not available purchase a 24" (60 cm) rather than a larger one.*
Quilting hoop	*Oval or round, either 14" (36 cm) or 18" (45 cm).*
Lap board	*10" x 14" (25.4 cm x 36 cm) piece of hardboard is best as it is light in weight and splinter-free. This is indispensable for working on your lap.*
Quilt batting	*100% polyester fibre, bonded.*
Materials	*Small-patterned calicos and ginghams preferably in polyester and cotton blends.*

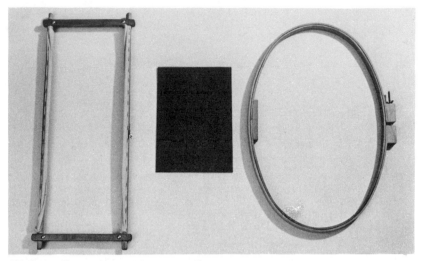

Fig. 1   Frames and lap board

HOW TO BUY AND PREPARE MATERIALS

Your choice of fabric will depend partly on the project for which you intend to use it. Many people still prefer to use 100% cotton and although many cottons wash well, some tend to wrinkle or shrink and the colour may bleed. For this reason, I prefer to work mainly with polyester and cotton blends which wash beautifully, do not wrinkle or shrink, are usually dye-fast and tend not to fade as readily as cotton. Small-patterned calicos and ginghams are best and today, with the renewed interest in quilting, these are in good supply in our stores.

Always launder all materials before using them. Wash and dry them as you normally would. If they are not dye-fast do not use them. This ensures that there will be no shrinkage or bleeding in future launderings and will make your finished article 100% washable. There is nothing more disappointing than to combine colours such as red and white in a pattern and then finding when it is laundered that the red bleeds into the white, ruining your work.

Lining materials should be made from the same blend as surface materials to ensure similar laundering qualities. They should also be washed before using.

HOW TO MAKE TEMPLATES (PATTERNS) FOR PATCHWORK AND APPLIQUÉ

Templates may be made from any piece of stiff cardboard or flat piece of plastic cut from plastic containers. If they are made from cardboard, a master pattern should be made and kept for making new templates in order to ensure accuracy. After tracing around a cardboard template several times the edges and corners become worn and seam lines are no longer accurate. It is then time to throw away the old, used template and make a new one from the master pattern.

There are two methods of making templates. One method includes a ¼″ (6 mm) seam allowance in the template so that the pencil line is the cutting line. If this method is used, the seam lines then have to be gauged ¼″ (6 mm) inside the cutting line. It is difficult to do this accurately for accuracy is of the utmost importance in sewing patches together in order to match the seam lines as perfectly as possible. If corners do not meet, it tends to destroy the beauty of the pattern and to look amateurish.

For this reason, I usually use the second method, which is to make the template *without a seam allowance*. This makes the pencil line traced around the template the seam line and it is very easy when sewing to match corners and seam lines for perfect accuracy. My students prefer this method to the first method.

In some instances in this book the seam allowance has been included in the pattern for ease of sewing, especially if the seam is to be machine-sewn and an accurate seam allowance can be gauged. In these cases I have noted on the pattern piece that the seam allowance is included.

When tracing the pattern piece on cardboard use a well-sharpened pencil; a blunt lead can cause a variation in pattern size. Cut out the cardboard template on the pencil lines. Then cut a small piece of medium grade sandpaper and, with your glue stick, paste it onto the back of the template. This will help to prevent the material from slipping when tracing the pattern. Write the name of the pattern on each template and the number of fabric pieces required for each shape. Your templates are now ready to use. Store each set of templates for a particular design in an envelope and mark the name of the design and the total number of templates on the outside. This will be the beginning of your pattern library.

Refer to the next two chapters for instructions on how to mark and cut your material for patchwork and appliqué.

Templates can also be purchased in a limited variety of shapes and sizes.

2 Patchwork

Anyone who is able to sew evenly and neatly by hand will enjoy patchwork. Patchwork is a term which originally included both piecework and appliqué. Today, however, it is commonly used to mean piecework only, as opposed to appliqué, and is the sewing together of fabrics in geometric shapes. Patchwork can be as simple as a combination of squares, as used in basic four or nine-patch patterns, or it can be a more complex combination of various geometric shapes.

When choosing your first design start with a simple pattern such as Nine Patch. Then gradually try more complex designs such as Shoo Fly and Jacob's Ladder, using triangles and squares, until you have gained enough experience to be able to sew the most intricate arrangements including small pieces and curves. There are numerous patterns made with simple squares and triangles from which to choose.

CUTTING THE PIECES FOR PATCHWORK

Patchwork patterns are always marked on the wrong side of the material so the seam line is visible when sewing the pieces. Lay the fabric on a flat, hard surface, wrong side up. Place the template on the fabric with the longest side on the straight grain of the fabric and with a sharp, medium-soft pencil trace around the edge of the template onto the fabric. Remember, you will be cutting ¼" (6 mm) outside the tracing line to allow for the seam allowance so leave ½" (1.3 cm) between each template tracing. Always remember the pencil line is the sewing line not the cutting line. If your cutting line is a little more or less than the ¼" (6 mm) outside the pencil line it will not matter. The important thing is to sew on the pencil line for absolute accuracy in order for the block to fit together properly and uniformly. Never cut more than one layer of material at a time. Material in layers is apt to slip.

SEWING PATCHWORK

I prefer to sew my patchwork pieces together by hand. Many of them are small and are more conveniently and accurately handled with hand sewing. Machine sewing tends to make a taut, hard line whereas hand sewing presents a softer appearance and is more easily quilted over.

The length of your thread should be approximately the distance from your elbow to your finger tips — long threads tend to tangle. Put a small knot on one end of the thread and sew along the seam line with a short running stitch — about 8 or 10 stitches to 1″ (2.5 cm). At the end of the seam take a couple of back stitches over the last stitch and clip the thread leaving a 1″ (2.5 cm) tail.

SEWING INSTRUCTIONS FOR BLOCKS BASED ON A SQUARE

Nine Patch Block

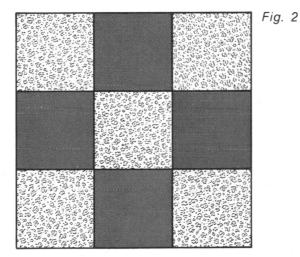

Fig. 2

Cut out a 4″ (10.1 cm) square template from cardboard. Cut five calico squares and four plain squares in a contrasting colour remembering to cut ¼″ (6 mm) outside the pencil line.

1. Lay out the squares of the block on a flat surface in the finished pattern. Always do this with any block before sewing it together to ensure sewing the pieces in the proper order.
2. With the right sides of the fabric facing, pin the sides of two squares together through the seam line, matching the corners. Ease in the remainder of the seam. Be careful not to stretch the edges.

Sew the squares as described above into three strips as illustrated below.

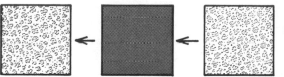

Fig. 3
Sew in strips.

3. Press the seams together in one direction, not open as in dressmaking. Press the seams of the next strip in the opposite direction if possible to form less bulk where joined at the corners and for easier quilting (Fig. 4). If a darker and lighter fabric are joined, press the seam toward the darker side.

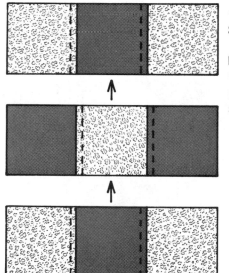

Fig. 4
Sew strips together.

Dotted lines are the direction of press lines for seam allowances.

4. Pin the first two strips together with seams matching precisely at corners and sides. Open out the strips and check to make sure corners are aligned before sewing. Sew on the third strip in the same manner. Press the block. You should now have a 12″ (30.5 cm) square plus ¼″ (6 mm) seam allowance on the outer edges.

Shoo Fly Block
The only difference between a simple Nine Patch block and the Shoo Fly pattern is the triangle used to form the corner squares. Sew the

two triangle pieces together first for these corner squares. Be careful not to stretch the bias edges. Then sew the squares in strips and finish as for Nine Patch.

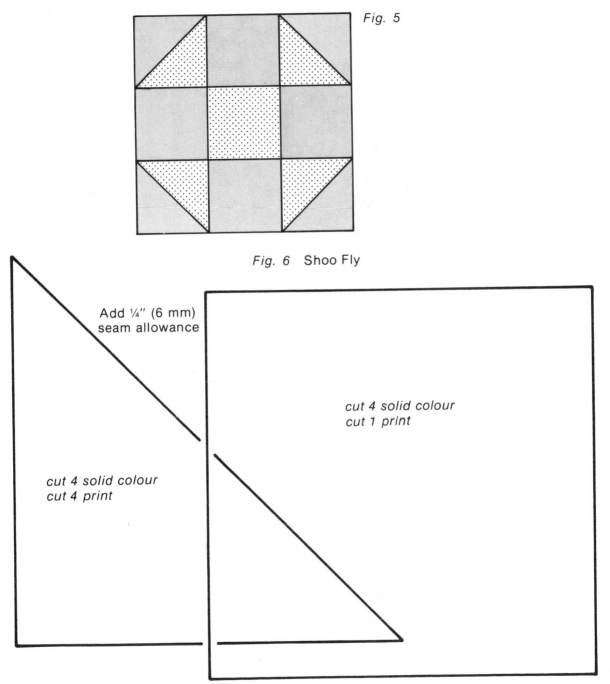

Fig. 5

Fig. 6   Shoo Fly

Add ¼" (6 mm)
seam allowance

cut 4 solid colour
cut 1 print

cut 4 solid colour
cut 4 print

Jacob's Ladder Block

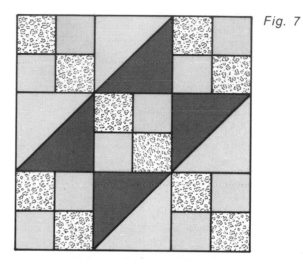

Fig. 7

This is another basic nine-patch block with the nine squares made up of smaller squares and triangles. To sew the corner and middle squares, first sew together two of the small squares, then the second

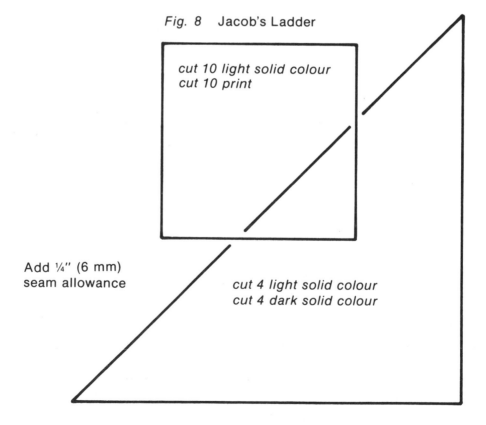

Fig. 8   Jacob's Ladder

cut 10 light solid colour
cut 10 print

Add ¼" (6 mm)
seam allowance

cut 4 light solid colour
cut 4 dark solid colour

two small squares. Sew these two strips together, matching the four centre seams where they meet to form the larger square. Sew the triangles together into squares. Lay out the squares in their proper order for the finished block. Sew the squares together into strips as directed for the Nine Patch Block.

Follow the basic steps as given above when putting together any patchwork block based on a square patch. When looking at a design, try to decide what its basic patchwork pattern is — four patch, nine or 16 patch. Once you have learned to unscramble the pattern and identify its basic design you are then able to easily sew together the various units forming the small square, sew the squares into rows, and the rows together to form the finished block.

SEWING INSTRUCTIONS FOR A HEXAGON SHAPE

Grandmother's Flower Garden (Plate 2)

Grandmother's Flower Garden design, made from hexagons, is an old English mosaic pattern typical of the upper class of the 18th and 19th centuries. It is still one of the popular patchwork patterns today. With the old method the complete quilt top was made of "flowers" composed of hexagons divided from the next "flower" by a neutral coloured "path" of hexagons surrounding each flower. The quilt was then quilted on a large frame.

The pattern may be adapted for lap quilting purposes by combining patchwork with appliqué as shown in the picture of my quilt (Plate 2). I appliquéd each flower to a 15½" (39.5 cm) square including the seam allowance.

Fig. 9   Grandmother's Flower Garden

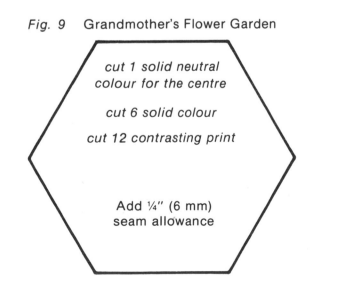

cut 1 solid neutral
colour for the centre

cut 6 solid colour

cut 12 contrasting print

Add ¼" (6 mm)
seam allowance

Each flower consists of one centre hexagon, six in the first row and 12 in the second row. Read the sections earlier in this chapter for cutting and sewing patchwork.

1. Starting with the centre hexagon, sew one side of each hexagon for the first row to a side of the centre one matching corners carefully and sewing only on the seam lines, not through the seam allowance Fig. 10(a).
2. Next sew the seams between these six hexagons (b).
3. Now sew the second row of hexagons to the first row (c).
4. Finally, sew the seams between the hexagons in the second row (d).

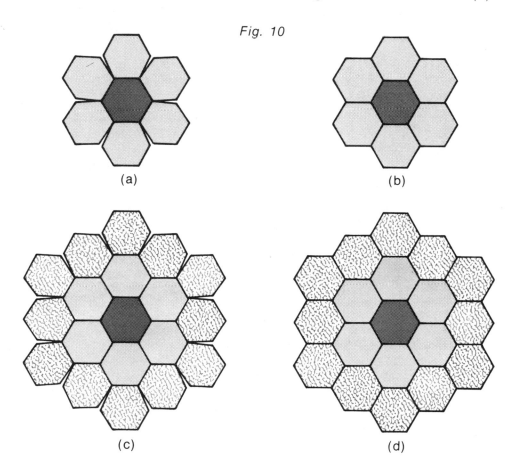

Fig. 10

(a)   (b)

(c)   (d)

If you are very careful to match all seam lines and corners and remember not to sew through the seam allowance, you will have no problem in uniformly fitting the hexagons together. Press the seams well. The flower is now ready to appliqué to a square. Follow the directions in the next chapter for sewing appliqué.

SEWING INSTRUCTIONS FOR A DIAMOND SHAPE

Blazing Star

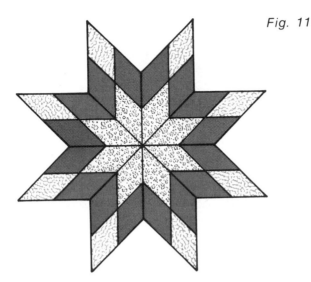

Fig. 11

Star patterns are always favourites with quilters and there are endless variations with as many names. Blazing Star is one of the traditional old-time variations that has been popular with quilters for many generations.

The eight points, each consisting of four diamond-shaped patches, are pieced together separately.

1. Cut out the required number of diamond pieces as indicated on the pattern. Read the sections in this chapter on cutting and sewing patchwork.

Fig. 12 Blazing Star

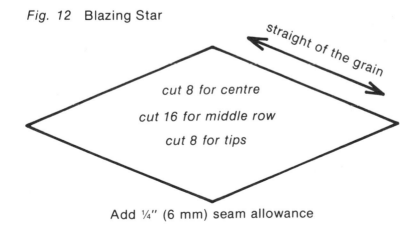

straight of the grain

cut 8 for centre

cut 16 for middle row

cut 8 for tips

Add ¼″ (6 mm) seam allowance

2. Sew the small diamond patches together in pairs as indicated by
   the arrows and then sew these two strips together across the
   middle. Carefully line up the seams at the intersection of the four
   diamond pieces.

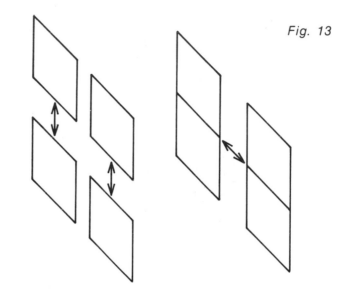

Fig. 13

3. When all eight points have been pieced together in this manner,
   sew four points together to form one-half of the star. Do not sew
   through the seam allowance at the ends of these seams as they need
   to be free to turn under when appliquéd.
4. Repeat for the second half of the star.
5. Sew the two halves together straight across the middle being
   careful again to line up all seams at the intersection in the centre
   of the star.

The star is now ready to be appliquéd to a 15½″ (39.5 cm) square or a
16½″ (42 cm) circle including seam allowances. When appliquéing it
is important to make the points sharp. First, fold the seam allowance
over the point and then fold in the seam allowances on either side as
shown in Fig. 14. Baste the seam allowance under all around the
edges before appliquéing. Follow the directions in the next chapter
for appliquéing.

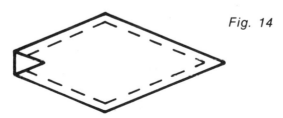

Fig. 14

3 Appliqué

Appliqué is the art of laying a fabric patch on a fabric background and then sewing the patch in place. If a simple pattern is chosen any beginner may be successful. In the early years, appliqué was usually reserved for "best" quilts because it was a more expensive method of patchwork. Appliqué was very often used for bridal quilts; this very special quilt was not sewn for a girl until after she became engaged, for bad luck was believed to come to any young lady for whom it was made before her engagement.

CUTTING THE PIECES FOR APPLIQUÉ

The cutting of appliqué pieces differs from patchwork in that the seam line is traced onto the right side of the material so that the seam allowance can be easily basted under on this line. Remember to cut ¼" (6 mm) outside the tracing line. The longest side of the template is usually placed on the straight grain of the fabric just as with patchwork. Appliquéd stems should be cut on the bias.

SEWING APPLIQUÉ

1. After tracing the pattern pieces onto the right side of the various materials, cut them out, remembering to add ¼" (6 mm) seam allowance outside the tracing line.
2. Baste the seam allowances under on the individual pieces on the seam line except where one piece of fabric is to be slipped under another. Clip curves where needed. DO NOT PRESS. If a lighter coloured material is to overlap a darker fabric it may be necessary to use a double thickness of the lighter material and treat it as one piece.

3. When all necessary edges have been basted under the pieces are ready to be appliquéd to the background. To find the centre of a square, fold two diagonal lines from the corners to the opposite corners and, using your fingers, press where the lines cross in the middle. Centre the pattern pieces around this point on the square and pin securely. Baste into place. DO NOT PRESS.

4. Blind stitch each piece fast using the appliqué stitch described below.

Appliqué Stitch

There are various stitches used to appliqué but I prefer to use a stitch that does not show on the surface which detracts from the design. It is a simple blind hemming stitch. The turned-under seam allowance on the piece to be appliquéd forms a "tube" or "tunnel" through which the needle will be slipped. This is the reason for not pressing the basted seam allowance flat. Slip the needle up through the background material 1/8″ (3 mm) into and along the tunnel. Then take another small stitch through the background fabric pulling up the thread until the knot is drawn up against the back of the material. Slip the needle back through and along the tunnel again 1/8″ (3 mm) before taking another short stitch in the background fabric. Continue in this manner to the end of the seam being careful not to pucker the stitching. The thread may be fastened on the back side with two back stitches leaving a 1″ (2.5 cm) tail or fastened off in the regular fashion with a knot. When all pieces are sewn fast the block is ready to be pressed.

A SUNBONNET SUE BLOCK (Plate 10)

One of the all-time favourite patterns which I start my students on is Sunbonnet Sue. Sometimes called Sunbonnet Baby or Little Dutch Girl, the pattern appeared in the early 1900s and was very popular by 1930. There are dozens of variations of the Sunbonnet Sue pattern and sampler quilts using only these variations have been made.

Materials Required for One Block of Sunbonnet Sue

Small piece of light coloured fabric for the hands
Fabric for the bonnet, dress and shoes
Bits of lace or trim to use around the edge of the bonnet or dress as desired
This pattern appliqués to a 15½″ (39.5 cm) square including seam allowance.

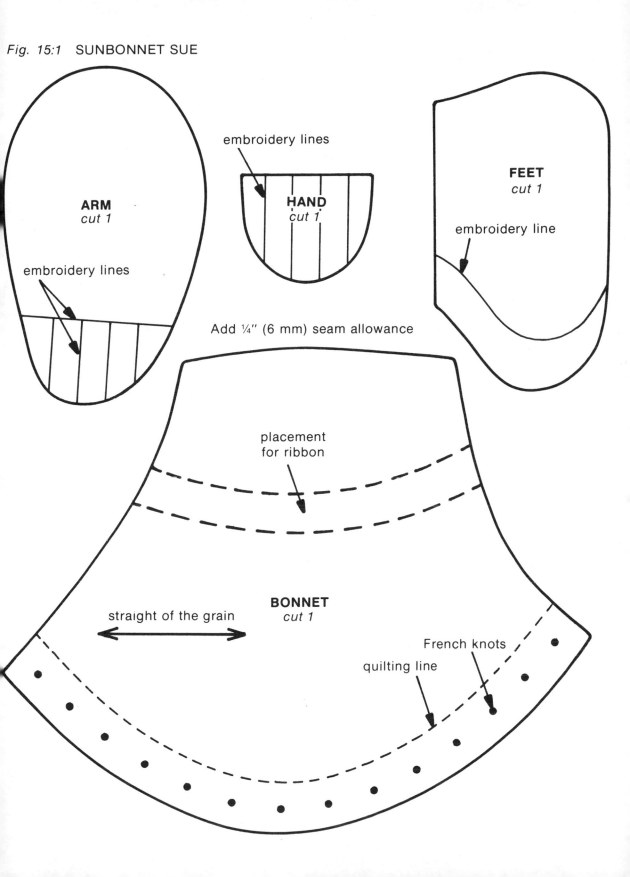

Fig. 15:1 SUNBONNET SUE

ARM
cut 1

embroidery lines

embroidery lines

HAND
cut 1

FEET
cut 1

embroidery line

Add ¼″ (6 mm) seam allowance

placement
for ribbon

BONNET
cut 1

straight of the grain

French knots

quilting line

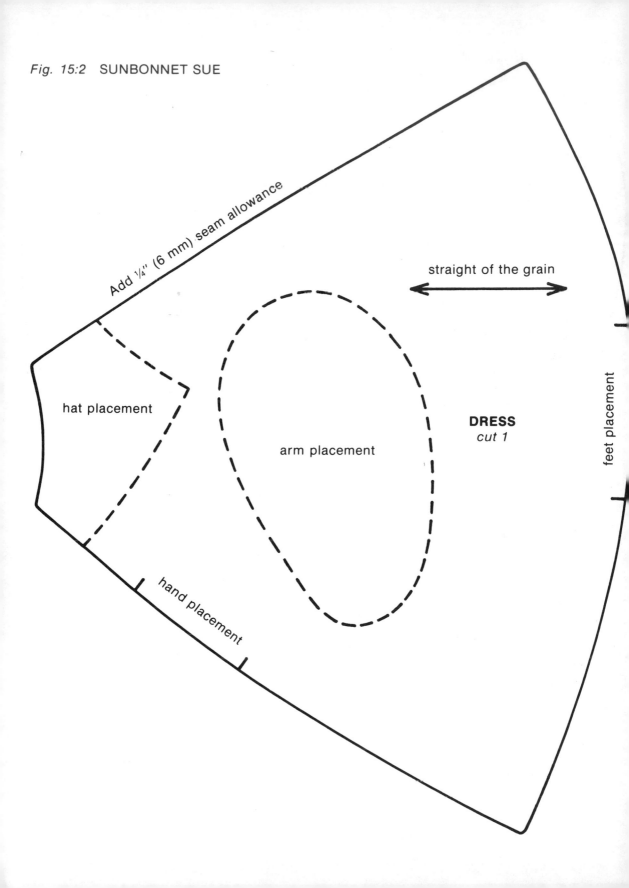

Fig. 15:2 SUNBONNET SUE

Add ¼" (6 mm) seam allowance

straight of the grain

hat placement

arm placement

DRESS
cut 1

feet placement

hand placement

Sewing Instructions

1. Cut out all the patches as directed on the pattern pieces following the instructions as given in this chapter for cutting and sewing appliqué.
2. Baste the seam allowances under on all the patches except the neck of the dress, where it slips under the bonnet, and the hand and the foot, where they slip under the dress.
3. After the pieces are appliquéd onto the square, press the block.
4. To make the ribbons on the bonnet, cut two pieces of bias material to match the dress, approximately 1" (2.5 cm) wide. Baste a ¼" (6 mm) seam allowance under and arrange on the bonnet. Lace or bias tape may be used instead if desired. Appliqué the ribbons to the bonnet and background piece.
5. Embroider the lines where indicated on hands and feet. Make the French knots on the bonnet.
6. The block is now ready to be quilted. Follow the instructions for quilting in Chapter 4, p. 28.

AN OVERALL SAM BLOCK (Plate 10)

Materials required for One Block of Overall Sam
Blue fabric for overalls
Small-check red gingham for shirt
Yellow fabric for straw hat
Bias strip for hat band
   This pattern appliqués to a 15½" (39.5 cm) square including the seam allowance.

Sewing Instructions
Cut out the pattern pieces as instructed earlier in this chapter. Follow the instructions for sewing appliqué. Baste the seam allowances under on all the patches except the top of the overall straps and the top and bottom edges of the shirt. The shirt and the overall straps are slipped under the edge of the straw hat. After appliquéing all the pieces to the background material cut a bias band for the straw hat and appliqué where indicated.

Fig. 16 OVERALL SAM

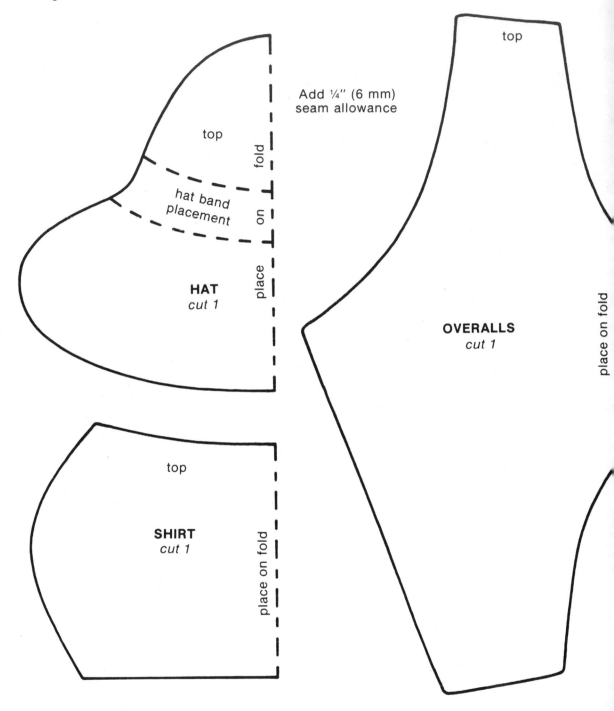

Add ¼" (6 mm)
seam allowance

top

fold

on

place

HAT
cut 1

hat band
placement

top

SHIRT
cut 1

place on fold

top

OVERALLS
cut 1

place on fold

4 Quilting on a Lap Frame

It is the actual quilting of the material which brings a block to life, giving an almost three-dimensional quality to a piece that was formerly flat and rather lifeless.

Pieced and appliquéd blocks are almost always quilted in lines parallel to the seams to emphasize the pattern. If the piecing is elaborate the quilting should be simple and the reverse is also true. If a plain square is used alternately with patchwork or appliqué, then an elaborate pattern may be quilted on the plain square but always in keeping with the pieced or appliquéd blocks, being careful that the design complements rather than overcomes.

Until the advent of synthetic quilt batting, cotton or wool batting was commonly used as well as flannelette sheets. Because cotton or wool batting tended to separate and pull apart with use, especially if laundered, quilting lines of necessity had to be very close together to hold the batting as securely as possible. Consequently, older quilts are heavily quilted with all-over quilting lines. Today, with our synthetic batting we do not need to be so concerned about their durability. Unquilted areas of up to 6″ (15 cm) present no problem, for synthetic batting is 100% washable or dry-cleanable and will not lump or mat.

TYPES OF QUILTING AND QUILTING PATTERNS

1. Outline quilting is the traditional and simplest style of quilting. It is a simple quilting line stitched ¼″ (6 mm) from the existing pattern lines. It is used on either patchwork or appliqué when you wish to accent the pattern without interference from the quilting lines. If it is possible to plan the quilting before pressing a patchwork block, then press the seams away from the side you plan to quilt as it is more difficult to quilt through several layers of material.

2. Blind quilting may be used when quilting stitches are required to hold the layers together but when quilting lines would detract from the block pattern. In such cases, quilt directly on top of the seam line (in the ditch) where stitches will be hidden.

3. All-over quilting designs are simple patterns which cover an entire area.

Fig. 17 All-over quilting designs

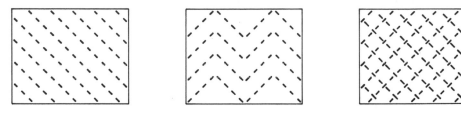

4. Chain patterns are quilting designs usually used for narrow strips or borders.

Fig. 18
Chain quilting
designs

5. Decorative designs are those used for quilting plain blocks and there is an unlimited supply of old favourites such as pineapples and feathers. But here is an opportunity for your imagination to supply you with an endless variety of your own creating.

MAKING YOUR OWN DESIGNS

Anyone can trace a quilting design from a book or magazine but it is only when you learn to make your own that your quilting truly reflects you. As well, it enables you to tailor a pattern to your required size.

Some of my students feel that this is an impossibility for them, for they do not consider themselves to be either artistic or creative. However, when I send them home with the task of creating a quilting pattern for the next class, the beauty of the designs with which they return is amazing, especially to themselves. One student said she thought that it was indeed an impossible task for her but when she began to work she discovered new ideas kept popping into her head until she had more ideas for designs than she would ever be able to use. This is truly one of the most creative and satisfying aspects of quilting.

Sources of Design

Our pioneer grandmothers did not have access to many prepared quilting patterns and so they turned to the world of nature around them — flowers, vines, trees, birds, leaves, feathers. They also looked in their own homes for other sources of inspiration and found dish patterns, bedspread and drape designs, or often the patterns in the materials with which they sewed. Glasses and plates were used to make varying sizes of circles which were sometimes overlapped for borders.

Making Designs

If you wish to make an elaborate design for a plain area, cut a square of paper the size of the area you wish to quilt. Fold the paper into four quarters: draw one-quarter of the pattern on one section, cut on the line through all four layers of paper and unfold. In this fashion you are able to make a symmetrical design very easily.

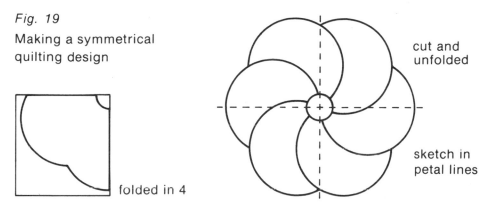

Fig. 19

Making a symmetrical quilting design

folded in 4

cut and unfolded

sketch in petal lines

Make a supply of small templates out of cardboard or plastic from old containers to keep on hand, i.e., ovals, circles, diamonds, or leaves in varying sizes, and use these to make your own patterns. A more elaborate design may be made with a stencil having several parts to it.

MARKING THE PATTERN ON THE MATERIAL

The quilting design is always marked on the fabric before the block is basted together with the batting and backing. Place the pressed block on a hard, flat surface and, using a medium-hard lead pencil, mark the design on the material as lightly as possible to prevent pencil lines showing after completion of quilting. An art gum may be used with some success to remove pencil lines after the quilting has been completed but this is not necessary if the design is put on lightly enough. On dark material use a white-leaded pencil. If a more elaborate design with many parts is being used then trace it on with dressmakers' carbon and a tracing wheel but be extremely careful as the carbon line will not wash out. Some carbon colours such as white are better to use than others such as red or blue.

Another method is to draw the design on paper and go over it with a black, felt-tipped marker. Then place the fabric to be quilted over this, pin carefully and trace the design with a fairly hard, sharp pencil. This can also be placed on a piece of glass with a light under it for better visibility.

I usually depend on cardboard or plastic templates and stencils for greatest success.

ASSEMBLING A BLOCK FOR QUILTING ON A LAP FRAME

1. Cut a lining square the same size as the completed block top.
2. Cut a piece of quilt batting the same size.
3. Lay out the lining, wrong side up, and place the batting over it, then the completed block top, right side up.
4. Pin the centre, corners and mid-sides through all layers, matching all raw edges.
5. Baste with a large stitch through all three layers, starting from the centre and following through to one corner and then from the

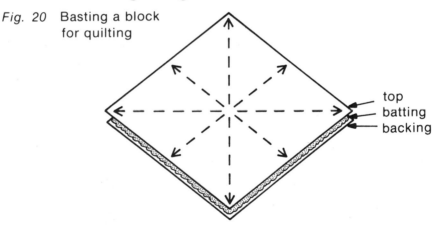

Fig. 20   Basting a block for quilting

top
batting
backing

centre to the opposite corner. This prevents the top from "wandering" on the batting. Continue in the same manner for the other two corners and then to each mid-side.
6. Firmly pin two sides of the basted block to the tapes on your tapestry frame. Adjust the tension on the block by turning one side of the frame and tightening. The block should be fairly taut but not too tight as this will make it difficult to get your needle through the material for even and small quilting stitches. Experience will teach you just how tight you need it. As you work

turn the block on one side of the frame and then the other, keeping the quilting area well away from the sides of the frame.

QUILTING ON A LAP FRAME (Plate 1)

The quilting stitch is a small running stitch sewn through the quilting lines on the block. At first your stitches will not be even or particularly small but this will come with practice. You may find the frame extremely awkward on a first try but persevere and soon you will be perfectly at home with it. Make sure that each stitch goes through the batting and catches the backing. The quilting pattern on the back when finished should, after some experience, look the same as that on the front. Your thread length should be approximately as long as the distance from the tip of your fingers to your elbow. Long threads are awkward for sewing. Make a small knot on one end of the thread, insert the threaded quilting needle through the top layer of material bringing the point out at the beginning of your line to be quilted. Pull the thread up until the knot reaches the surface. With a sharp little tug, pull the knot through into the batting where it will be buried and not show on either the back or front.

Quilt toward yourself, holding the frame on your lap with one hand underneath, and using your finger to help guide the needle. With short running stitches take two or three small, even stitches on your needle, making sure you have caught the lining and pull through firmly but not so tightly that it will gather the material. Continue in this manner taking five to six stitches to 1″ (2.5 cm) (your stitches will gradually become smaller with experience) until you reach the end of the quilting line or you run out of thread. Do not knot the end of the thread in quilting as it tends to pucker the material. Instead take two little back stitches over your last quilting stitch, then run the needle with the thread through the top surface into your batting bringing the needle out about 1″ (2.5 cm) from where it was inserted. Clip the thread close to the material. This allows the end of the thread to become buried in the batting making it invisible from either side. Try to finish a quilting line at a corner or in a place that is not too obvious.

Never quilt closer than ½″ (1.3 cm) from the edge of any block. This allows for the ¼″ (6 mm) seam allowance when you sew the blocks or pieces together.

When the quilting is completed, remove the block from your frame and carefully pull out the basting stitches. It is now complete with quilting to be sewn to another block for a quilt, made into a pillow or used in the project for which you have designed it.

5 Pillows

Whether functional or decorative, pillows are a welcome addition to any home. Quilted pillows may be made of either patchwork or appliqué and can be both practical and ornamental. They make attractive and appreciated gifts. I make my pillows with either a patchwork or appliqué front and the backs from a plain material with an ornately quilted design on it, usually in a contrasting colour of thread. For instance, a pillow front made in brown and sand patchwork could have a quilted pattern in sand thread on a brown fabric for its back. As well as adding extra interest, this makes it reversible with completely different decorating results.

Fig. 21   Pillow fronts

Pillow backs

A pillow consists of two quilted blocks, one for the front and one for the back, sewn together. The easiest filling is a stuffing of polyester fibrefill which can be purchased in bags and is commonly used to stuff children's toys. If a purchased pillow form is used then your block sizes will need to conform to its measurements. Foam rubber chips may also be used if desired but they are more satisfactory if a separate pillow form is made to place inside the quilted covering. Since the backing on each quilted block will be inside the pillow it will not matter what is used for it as long as it is the same blend as the top surfaces for washing purposes. Since all the materials used are laundered and if the filling is of polyester fibre, the pillow can be easily washed when necessary in your washing machine by using warm water and a gentle cycle. Dry it in your dryer on a low setting, removing when still slightly damp. Allow it to sit until completely dry.

Pillow covers for feather pillows or other unwashable forms should be closed with a zipper on one side so the cover may be removed for washing. This leaves the back free to do decorative quilting and allows the pillow to be reversible.

When choosing pillow fabrics, don't forget about using silks and heavier materials such as velvet and corduroy, the heavier materials being particularly effective in crazy patchwork.

TO MAKE A PILLOW OF QUILTED BLOCKS (Plate 3)

First sew together a block of appliqué or patchwork. If desired, a border may be sewn around the edges. Complete the block by quilting it on your frame as directed in Chapter 4, p. 28. Prepare an ornately quilted block in the same size for the back. A frill or piping may be added as you sew the pillow together. If you wish a more tailored appearance then sew the blocks together without these additions.

TO MAKE A PILLOW WITH A FRILL

First complete a front and back block for the pillow. The narrowest pillow ruffle should not be less than 3″ (7.6 cm) wide when finished, otherwise the frill tends to look skimpy rather than luxurious. I make the ruffle of the same coloured fabric as the back of the pillow. It should be made from one strip of material folded double so there is no hem on the outside edge.

1. Cut or tear a strip or strips of material for the frill 6½″ (16.5 cm) wide and double the distance around the pillow in length, plus ¼″ (6 mm) seam allowances for each seam in the length of the frill

plus 4″ (10.1 cm) to allow a pleat at each corner. Pleats allow the frill to lie flat at the corners.

2. Sew the strips together into one long strip and then join the ends to form a circle. Press the seams open. With wrong sides together, fold the strip in half lengthwise with the two raw edges even. Press well.

3. Machine sew two lines of gathering stitches close together in the ¼″ (6 mm) seam allowance around the total circle and through both layers of material.

4. With pins, divide the frill into four quarters. Lay the frill on top of the quilted pillow front, right sides together and raw edges even. Pin each quarter marker to a corner of the pillow top.

5. Pull up the gathering thread on each side to fit the pillow top, distributing the gathers evenly and making a ¼″ (6 mm) pleat on either side of each corner. Pin carefully, making sure the raw edges of the frill and pillow top are even. For a neater appearance, round the corners slightly rather than trying to make a square corner. Baste if desired.

6. Machine stitch the gathered frill to the pillow top ¼″ (6 mm) from the edge all around.

7. With right sides together, place the block for the pillow back on top of the frill and pillow front matching corners. Pin or baste securely.

8. Turn the pillow cover over with the wrong side of the pillow front on top. Following the seam line already sewn for the frill, machine stitch all around the block leaving an opening on one side for stuffing and turning.

9. Turn the pillow right side out and stuff. Sew opening closed by hand with a slip stitch.

TO SEW A PILLOW WITH PIPING OR CORDING

By using a zipper foot on your sewing machine, cording can be easily made with purchased filler cord covered with one of the fabrics used in the pillow. Measure the distance around the pillow and allow several extra inches. Allow at least a ½″ (1.3 cm) seam allowance for piping as it is much easier to work with. Sew the piping on in the same manner as the frill, rounding the corners and overlapping the ends. Finish the pillow in the same fashion as with a frill.

See Chapter 6, p. 42, for pillows and floor cushions in the Log Cabin Design.

6　Log Cabin Pattern

Another favourite pattern popular in both England and America since the middle of the 19th century is the Log Cabin. There are many claims about its origin but since mummified cats wrapped in this design, made by the Ancient Egyptians, are in the British Museum it would seem to prove that it is a very old pattern indeed.

The block is composed of a central square around which strips of material are built, edges overlapping. Light coloured fabrics are used on two sides and dark coloured fabrics on the opposite sides (Plate 4). Traditionally, the centre square is red, representing the cabin fire while the light side of the block is the bright side of the cabin and the dark side the shadowed part. The strips represent the logs.

CHOICE OF MATERIALS FOR LOG CABIN BLOCKS

Each Log Cabin block is made from a centre square and 20 strips of material, 10 light in colour in the same tone and 10 dark in the same tone. The projects shown in this book are made from 20 different fabrics. They may also be made from 10 different fabrics by using the same material for two strips instead of using a different fabric for each.

When buying the fabrics look for small-print calicos as large prints do not show to advantage. I like to include in my assortment one piece of plain broadcloth in both the light and dark colour as well as a gingham and a dot or a stripe. The effect is greater if you intersperse these with small prints. Buy colours or tones that will keep your contrast high for best effect.

Since the sewing of the strips in straight lines is essential to the resulting squareness of the block, I have my students use gingham for their lining material. This allows the quilter to use the straight lines of the gingham as a guide for sewing the strips on in perfectly straight lines and greatly simplifies the whole sewing process. Gingham also seems appropriate as a lining for a Log Cabin block.

PREPARATION OF MATERIALS

As in all quilting projects, wash and dry all the materials before you begin to use them. This includes the lining material as well. As uniform strips with straight edges are essential in building square Log Cabin blocks, the easiest way to prepare your strips, assuming you are using cotton blends, is to tear them on the straight of the grain of the fabric. Since some materials tear to better advantage than others, allow approximately 1/16" (1.5 mm) more in width than the 1½" (3.8 cm) measurement for each strip. Remove any extra threads on the sides of the strips and press flat. You now have a straight, flat edge to work with.

MATERIALS REQUIRED FOR ONE LOG CABIN BLOCK

All measurements include a ¼" (6 mm) seam allowance.

Twenty strips of fabric, measuring 1½" x 45" (3.8 cm x 1.14 m), consisting of 10 light coloured fabrics in the same tone and 10 dark coloured fabrics in the same tone. This will be sufficient to make the surface for five Log Cabin blocks.

In addition to the strips for EACH block you will need:
One 2½" (6.3 cm) square of plain fabric for the centre
One 12½" (31.8 cm) square of quilt batting
One 12½" (31.8 cm) square of lining material, preferably gingham

SEWING A LAP QUILTED LOG CABIN BLOCK

Log Cabin blocks constructed in the traditional manner used a foundation square, often of muslin. The small square was tacked in the middle of the foundation piece and the strips were then built around the centre. After all the blocks had been sewn, they were then set together in a design of the quilter's choice. The top was put into a large frame with a lining and usually an interlining and quilted along each strip.

The whole process is made very much easier with our method of lap quilting. Not only do the blocks have the batting incorporated into them but one stitching completes the block as well. No further quilting is needed.

1. It requires a little planning to ensure having sufficient material from the 20 strips to make five blocks. The strips which you have

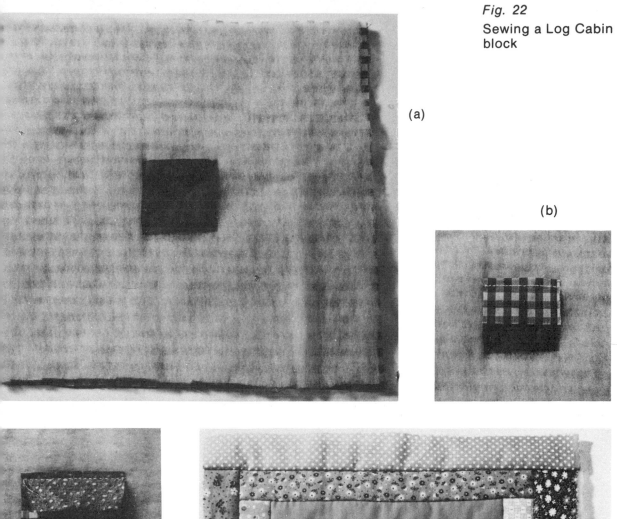

(a)

Fig. 22
Sewing a Log Cabin block

(b)

(c)

(d)

used for the short strips in one block should be used for the
longer strips in another block and vice versa. Watch the length of
your strips and this will ensure your having enough material to
sew all blocks.

2. Lay your lining square wrong side up on a hard, flat surface. I
   use my lap board as it is more comfortable to sit in my easy chair
   than to sit at a table.

3. Place the square of quilt batting on top.

4. Place the small square for the centre of the block in the middle of
   the batting and lining. Measure very carefully to make absolutely
   sure it is exactly 5" (12.7 cm) from all sides of the small square to
   the edge of the lining Fig. 22(a). The lines on the gingham
   lining will help you to line it up squarely. Pin all four corners
   with pins on the diagonal pointing toward each corner for ease of
   sewing over them.

5. Choose which colour of strip you are going to begin your sewing
   and with each succeeding block remember to always start with
   that colour.

6. Place the strip, right sides together, along one side of the centre
   square with raw edges matching. Sew the strip across the side of
   the square with a small running stitch in a ¼" (6 mm) seam,
   sewing through all thicknesses of strip, square, batting and lining
   (b). As you sew, taking two or three small running stitches on
   your needle, check on the back lining to make sure your seam is
   running parallel to the lines on the gingham. Fasten off the end
   of the seam with two back stitches and clip the thread leaving a
   1" (2.5 cm) tail which will embed itself in the batting.

7. With scissors, carefully cut off the remainder of the strip but be
   careful not to clip off the tail of thread you have left. Turn the
   sewn strip out onto the batting and flatten. With pins pointing
   toward the raw edge pin the strip securely making sure that the
   gingham lining is also smooth and flat under it.

8. Turn the block 90° in a clockwise fashion.

9. Using another strip of the same colour, apply in the same fashion
   sewing across the side of the small square and the end of the first
   strip (c).

10. Fold out this strip and pin well, again making sure the lining is
    smooth and not wrinkled.

11. Now you are ready to sew on two strips of the second colour on
    the remaining two sides of the square. Sew them in exactly the
    same fashion as the first two with each strip overlapping the ends
    of the previous strips. When you have completed the first row
    around the small square you will begin a second row of "logs"

starting again with the first colour. By using two strips of the first colour and then two of the second colour you will end up with two sides of all light colour and the opposite two sides of all dark colours. (See Fig. 22(d), p. 35.)

12. When you sew on the last four strips there will be four places where the ends of the seams meet the outer edge of the block. Do not sew the last ¾" (1.9 cm) of these four seams through the batting and lining but only join the edges of the two strips together leaving the batting and lining free. When sewing the blocks together you will need to have this seam allowance free as described in the section in Chapter 8, "To Sew Together Lap Quilted Blocks."

HELPFUL HINTS ON LOG CABIN CONSTRUCTION

1. Make sure you are sewing straight lines — constantly check the seams on the under-side to make sure they are parallel with the lines on the gingham lining.
2. Measure each strip after it is sewn for accuracy of width before sewing on the next strip on that side. If one strip becomes a little narrow or a little too wide, compensate with the next strip on that side by taking a wider or narrower seam. This way the error is corrected quickly without being very obvious and the block will end up square.

PROJECTS USING THE LOG CABIN PATTERN

LOG CABIN QUILTS (Plate 4)

The earliest Log Cabin quilts were often made from woolens for warmth but gradually lighter materials came to be used, sometimes even silks.

The final design of the quilt depends on the arrangement of blocks with their light and dark sides. Depending on their placement, such patterns as Barn-Raising, Straight Furrow, Path Through the Woods, and Sunshine and Shadow are formed. If the fabrics used for Log Cabin blocks are rich in colour then the design chosen to sew them together does not particularly matter for all are quite lovely. It is probably one of the fastest quilts to make for, traditionally, it does not require a border but may be finished with just a binding around the outer edge. In the quilt pictured I chose to use a 6" (15.2 cm) border all around in order to add 12" (30.5 cm) to the width of my quilt. If I had added another block instead, it would have put my chosen design, Sunshine and Shadow, off-centre.

Except for sewing on the lining for the border (the top of the border was done by hand) and one edge of the binding, the quilt was completely made in my lap on my lap board. It was sewn mostly in spare moments while dinner was cooking or while watching a television program. For that reason it is hard to estimate the length of time required to make such a quilt but a rough estimate is 250 to 300 hours.

Size

First of all, decide on how large a quilt you want. Read in Chapter 8, "Planning Your Quilt." Decide whether you want to use a border or just a binding around the edge. The blocks sew into a finished 12" (30.5 cm) square so divide your measurements by 12 (30.5) and you will know the total number of blocks you will need.

Materials Required

STRIPS FOR THE LOGS Before beginning your quilt read the sections at the beginning of this chapter on choice of materials, preparation and the amount of material required for one block of Log Cabin. Since each "set" (20 strips, each measuring 1½" (3.8 cm) wide) will make five blocks, divide the total number of blocks by five and you will then know how many sets you will require. For instance, if you decide you require 40 blocks, divide this by five and you will know that you need eight sets. This would work out to exactly 12" (30.5 cm) of each fabric but since you want to allow a little extra for tearing, you will need to add on a few extra inches. Also, since most stores do not tear the fabric when purchased, you often lose a small amount of fabric at either end by the time you tear off an end to straighten it. You will need to allow enough extra material on one of your plain fabrics to cut the small squares for the centres of the blocks. You will also need to allow extra for the fabric to be used as binding. If you should decide on a border then purchase the material for it at the same time since dye lots do differ.

LINING If you are making 40 blocks, then you will need 40 12½" (31.8 cm) squares of gingham. You can easily work out the amount of gingham required by cutting three squares across 45" (1.14 m) wide material. For 40 blocks you would need 13 rows of three squares each, plus one square. Therefore, buy enough for one more row — 175" (445 cm) or approximately 5 yd. (4.45 m) of 45" (1.14 m) wide material. This will allow you enough material for straightening at both ends if necessary. If you are using a border remember to allow sufficient lining material for it as well.

BATTING I like to buy packaged quilt batts rather than buying batting by the yard as the quality is inclined to be better and it is usually of a more uniform thickness. One quilt batt is sufficient to make one average-sized double-bed quilt.

Setting a Log Cabin Quilt

After deciding on the size of the quilt, you may decide on the design for setting the blocks. If you can decide on the design before sewing the blocks you can then refer to adjoining blocks as you sew and avoid using a particular fabric strip on the outside of one block if it is used on an adjoining one. If you cannot decide on the set of your blocks before they are sewn, then complete the required number of blocks as directed in this chapter under "Sewing a Lap Quilted Log Cabin Block," p. 34, and lay them out in various ways to help you decide. To sew the blocks together refer to the directions in Chapter 8, "To Sew Together a Lap Quilted Quilt," p. 76.

Border

If you should decide to use a border refer to Chapter 8, "Borders," p. 78. The same general rules will apply but the corners will look more in keeping with the "log" design of the quilt if you sew the corners squarely, rather than mitring them.

Binding

A binding 1" (2.5 cm) wide when finished may be sewn on all around to finish the quilt either with or without the border. The binding will also better reflect the log pattern of the blocks if sewn squarely on the corners rather than being mitred. Refer to Chapter 8, "Bindings," p. 79, for cutting and sewing instructions.

LOG CABIN BAGS (Plate 5)

Handbags sewn in the Log Cabin pattern can be made in the two different sizes as pictured by using four blocks for the larger one and two for the smaller bag. These bags are not only handy to have for your own use but they make beautiful gifts for almost anyone. The small bag is particularly suited for use as a summer purse. The

Fig. 23

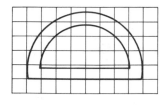
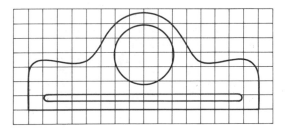

1 square = 1" (2.5 cm)

wooden handles for these bags were made by my husband from ¼″ (6 mm) birch plywood and seem particularly appropriate for the Log Cabin pattern.

Materials Required for a Log Cabin Bag Composed of Four Blocks
These bags are equally attractive in colour combinations other than the reds and blues which I have used.

Twenty strips of various materials, measuring 1½″ x 45″ (3.8 cm x 1.14 cm) — 10 in blue and 10 in red. Read the sections on the choice and preparation of materials at the beginning of this chapter.
Four 2½″ (6.3 cm) red squares for the centre of the blocks
Four 12½″ (31.8 cm) squares of quilt batting
Four 12½″ (31.8 cm) squares of red or blue gingham for lining
Two strips of gingham, measuring 3″ x 26″ (7.6 cm x 66 cm), in the same colour as the lining to fasten the bag to the handles

Sewing Instructions
1. Make four Log Cabin blocks as directed in this chapter under "Sewing a Lap Quilted Log Cabin Block." Join two blocks together along one side as directed in Chapter 8, "To Sew Together a Lap Quilted Quilt," p. 76. Join the remaining two blocks together in the same manner. Now join both strips together along the longest edge. This seam will form the bottom of the bag.
2. Fold the two sides right sides together. Sew the side seams to within 4″ (10.1 cm) of the tops in the same manner as the centre and bottom seams were sewn — that is "log" surfaces together,

Fig. 24

overlap the batting, turn in the lining material and blind stitch it together. The 4″ (10.1 cm) opening at the top will allow for easy opening of the bag as shown in the picture below. Reinforce the end of the seam at the opening with several overcast stitches for strength.

3. Trim back the batting on the edges of this opening.

4. On each side of the opening turn in the edge of the lining and the "log" front ¼″ (6 mm) toward each other and blind stitch around the opening.

5. With right sides together, pin one long strip to the top edge of one side of the bag turning the ends of the strip in 1″ (2.5 cm) so they will be even with either side of the bag. For strength, machine stitch a ¼″ (6 mm) seam across the strip and through all thicknesses of the blocks. Reinforce both ends of the seam for strength.

6. Sew the second strip to the other side of the bag in the same manner.

7. Slip the raw edge of one strip through the slot on one wooden handle, pulling it toward the inside of the bag until the edge of the Log Cabin pattern rests on the top of the slot. This will prevent the strip from showing on the outside of the bag.

8. On the inside of the bag turn under the raw edge of the strip about 1¼″ (3.2 cm) and securely whip stitch it in place. Use the lines of the gingham to make a straight seam. This will still leave sufficient room for the handle to turn easily inside its casing at the top of the bag. Repeat on the second side of the bag. Your bag is now ready to use.

Materials Required for a Log Cabin Bag Composed of Two Blocks

Twenty strips of various materials, measuring 1½″ x 24″ (3.8 cm x 61 cm) — 10 blue and 10 red. Read the sections on choice and preparation of materials at the beginning of this chapter.

Two 2½″ (6.3 cm) red squares for the centre of the blocks

Two 12½″ (31.8 cm) squares of quilt batting

Two 12½″ (31.8 cm) squares of red or blue gingham for lining

Two strips of gingham, each measuring 3″ x 14″ (7.6 cm x 35.5 cm), in the same colour as the lining to fasten the bag to the handles

Sewing Instructions

1. Make two Log Cabin blocks as directed in this chapter under "Sewing a Lap Quilted Log Cabin Block."

2. Using two blocks instead of four, follow the directions given for the large Log Cabin bag above. The strips fastening the bag to the handle will be pulled through the small handle and finished on the inside in the same manner as for the larger bag.

Optional Inside Pocket

Since I use my small bag for a summer purse, I find an inside pocket very useful. After completing the two blocks and before sewing them together, I whip stitch a piece of gingham to the lining of one of the blocks. I then hand sew a zipper in to close the pocket. Be careful not to let your stitches come through to the front of the block where they would show. Finish your bag as instructed above.

LOG CABIN PILLOW AND FLOOR CUSHIONS (Plate 3)

Log Cabin is a particularly adaptable pattern for making pillows. It blends beautifully with colonial or country decor. These pillows are equally lovely whether made in reds and blues, greens and browns, or golds and browns. Keep your colour contrast high.

Materials Required for a 12″ (30.5 cm) Pillow

You will need one Log Cabin block. For material requirements refer to the beginning of this chapter under "Materials Required for One Log Cabin Block" and follow the directions in this chapter for "Sewing a Lap Quilted Log Cabin Block." You will also need an ornately quilted block in the same size for the back. An alternative is to use two blocks of Log Cabin, one on either side. Refer to Chapter 5, p. 31, for directions for sewing and stuffing the pillow either with or without a frill or piping.

LOG CABIN MINI-SQUARES PILLOW

This pillow makes up into a 12″ (30.5 cm) pillow but consists of four 6″ (15.2 cm) blocks sewn together. This is a great way to use up left-over strips from other projects since each block uses only two strips on each side of the centre square and the same fabrics do not have to be used in each of the four blocks.

Materials Required

Four 2½″ (6.3 cm) squares for the centres
Eight 1½″ (3.8 cm) strips of various fabrics in various lengths, four in one
  colour tone and four in a second colour tone (for each block)
Four 6½″ (16.5 cm) squares of gingham for lining
Four 6½″ (16.5 cm) squares of quilt batting
One 12½″ (31.8 cm) ornately quilted block for the back

Sewing Instructions

Sew each small block as directed earlier in this chapter under "Sewing a Lap Quilted Log Cabin Block" using only two strips on each side of each centre square. Sew the blocks together into a square as follows. Machine sew with right sides of the blocks together and through all layers of both blocks. The seams will be inside the pillow and will not show. Finish the pillow as directed in Chapter 5, p. 31.

LOG CABIN FLOOR CUSHION

Young people love floor cushions and they are particularly nice in front of the fireplace. Again, Log Cabin is an especially good pattern to use for this purpose. Since the cover will probably need to be washed often, it is best to make or buy a separate pillow form for the inside.

Materials Required for a 24″ (61 cm) Floor Cushion

The cushion consists of four 12″ (30.5 cm) blocks of Log Cabin. Four quilted blocks of any patchwork pattern could be used to equal advantage. Read the sections on choice and preparation of materials at the beginning of this chapter. For fabric requirements for four blocks of Log Cabin refer to the beginning of this chapter under "Materials Required for One Log Cabin Block."

You will also need:

One 24½″ (62.2 cm) square of a heavy material for the back of the cushion. (Jute or corduroy are good choices as they will withstand the wear and tear of contact with the floor.) Be sure to wash the material first to ensure it will neither shrink nor bleed colour.

One 24″ (61 cm) pillow form either purchased or made at home and stuffed with sufficient polyester fibrefill of the type used for stuffing toys to fill the form fairly firmly. Alternatively, approximately 2 lbs. (1 kg) of shredded foam may also be used.

One 24″ (61 cm) zipper

Sewing Instructions

Sew four blocks of Log Cabin as directed in this chapter under "Sewing a Lap Quilted Log Cabin Block." Sew the blocks together as directed for the preceding Mini-Squares Pillow. This is the cushion top and should measure 24½″ (62.2 cm) square. Sew it to the pillow back on three sides. Turn it right side out. Sew in the zipper on the fourth side. Slip the pillow form inside. This will permit easy removal of the cover for washing.

LOG CABIN PLACE-MATS (Plate 6)

Log Cabin place-mats are a particularly nice gift for anyone who has a colonial theme in their dining area and are especially nice for a cottage. Since a place-mat needs to be rectangular, all that is required to adapt the square Log Cabin block is to use a rectangular piece for the centre instead of the usual square.

Materials Required for One Log Cabin Place-Mat

Review the sections dealing with choice of materials and preparation at the beginning of this chapter.

Sixteen strips of material measuring 1½″ x 45″ (3.8 cm x 1.14 cm) — eight in yellow, eight in brown. This should be sufficient to make four place-mats if the materials left over from the short strips in one mat are used for the longer strips in another. Read "Sewing a Lap Quilted Log Cabin Block" in this chapter, p. 34.

Two strips, measuring 2″ x 13½″ (5 cm x 34.3 cm) for each mat — one yellow and one brown. (These also act as binding for the two ends of the outside edges.)

Two strips, measuring 2″ x 19½″ (5 cm x 49.5 cm) for each mat — one yellow and one brown. (These also act as binding for the two long sides of the outside edges.)

One rectangle, measuring 2½″ x 8½″ (6.3 cm x 21.5 cm), for the centre — either yellow or brown

One piece of quilt batting, measuring 12″ x 18″ (30.5 cm x 45.7 cm)

One piece of brown or yellow gingham, measuring 12″ x 18″ (30.5 cm x 45.7 cm)

Sewing Instructions

Place the gingham, wrong side up, on a flat surface. I use my lap board. Place the quilt batting on top. Centre the small rectangle exactly in the middle of the lining and batting. Pin securely. Proceed in the usual fashion described in this chapter under "Sewing a Lap Quilted Log Cabin Block" working around the centre rectangle until four strips have been sewn on all sides. The 2″ (5 cm) outside strips may now be sewn on in the same manner as the others. To complete the place-mat, turn the strips over the edge to act as a binding. They will overlap on the back by ¾″ (1.9 cm). You may mitre the corners on the back side for a neater finish if desired. Pin well. Turn the edge of the strip under ¼″ (6 mm) and hem into place.

LOG CABIN HOT MAT COVERS (Plate 7)

Hot mat covers made to match your place-mat set add a real touch to your table with very little work. These covers will fit a 7″ (17.7 cm) square metal-surfaced stove and counter asbestos mat which may be purchased in many stores. The covers are made in pillowcase fashion with the asbestos mat slipping inside. They should be made a little larger than the purchased mat for easy insertion.

Materials Required for a 7¼" (18.4 cm) Log Cabin Mat Cover
One 1¾" (4.5 cm) square for the centre
Sixteen strips of material, eight in dark tones, eight in light tones, measuring 1¼" (3.2 cm) wide and varying in length up to 8" (20.2 cm)
One 7¾" (19.7 cm) square of gingham for backing
One 7¾" (19.7 cm) square of quilt batting
One 7¾" (19.7 cm) square of matching broadcloth for the back of the "pillowcase"

Sewing Instructions
Sew the Log Cabin block in the usual fashion following the directions in this chapter, "Sewing a Lap Quilted Log Cabin Block," using four strips on each side of the centre square. The block should measure 7¾" (19.7 cm) square when finished. On one side of the block turn in the raw edges of the last strip and the gingham backing toward each other and blind stitch the edge together. This is the side for the finished opening. Turn one edge of the square for the back of the "pillowcase" under ¼" (6 mm) and sew. Place the back square and the Log Cabin block with right sides and finished edges together. Match the corners and sides. Machine stitch the three raw edges ¼" (6 mm) from the edge, leaving the finished side open. Trim the batting if necessary. Turn it right side out. The hot mat may now be slipped into the cover.

LOG CABIN SHOE BAG (Plate 5)
If you enjoy sewing the Log Cabin pattern then here is another way to use the design in making yourself or your friends an attractive and useful bag for carrying shoes. For other shoe bags refer to Chapter 7, p. 58.

Materials Required for One Log Cabin Shoe Bag 12" x 14" (30.5 cm x 35.5 cm)
Twenty strips of material, 10 in red tones and 10 in blue tones, measuring 1½" x 36" (3.8 cm x 91.5 cm)
Two 2½" (6.3 cm) red squares
Two 2½" (6.3 cm) blue squares
Two gingham lining pieces measuring 12½" x 14½" (31.8 cm x 36.9 cm)
Two rectangles of quilt batting measuring 12½" x 14½" (31.8 cm x 36.9 cm)
One 26" (66 cm) length of bias tape (same colour as lining)
One 39" (1 m) length of cording in blue or red

Sewing Instructions
In order to make the bag rectangular and long enough to hold shoes,

two squares are placed in the centre and the strips are built around them. Lay out one gingham rectangle wrong side up. Place one piece of batting on top. Place one red square exactly 5" (12.7 cm) from one end and centre it between the two long sides of the gingham rectangle. Pin securely. Lay a blue square on top of the red, right sides together. Sew a seam ¼" (6 mm) from the edge with a running stitch through both squares, batting, and gingham across the side which is in the centre of the rectangle. Turn the blue square out flat onto the batting. The two squares should form a rectangle equidistant from all sides of the gingham rectangle. Using this as the centre to build your log strips around, continue as directed earlier in this chapter under "Sewing a Lap Quilted Log Cabin Block." Make a second block in exactly the same manner. For sewing and finishing the bag follow the directions in Chapter 7, "Quilted Shoe Bag," p. 59.

7 Quilting Small Projects

There is almost no limit to the number and variety of articles that you can make using patchwork, appliqué and quilting techniques. These are the "fun" items with which to let your imagination run away. In this chapter I have tried to include articles that will set your imagination to work. Expand on the ideas and come up with your own projects and designs. These articles are not only useful but they also make great gifts for special occasions — Christmas, birthdays, showers and weddings, etc.

PLACE-MATS (Plate 6)

Place-mats are an all-time favourite for gifts. Several of my students have made them for shower and birthday gifts. Complete the set with a matching centre-table runner and hot-mat covers following the directions given later in this chapter (Plate 8). I use a polyester and cotton blend fabric for these sets. They wash beautifully and require no pressing. If grease stains remain in the fabric, add a little liquid ammonia to your wash water and launder as usual. The spots will disappear.

PATCHWORK PLACE-MATS

A place-mat should measure at least 12″ x 18″ (30.5 cm x 45.7 cm) when finished. One of the easiest place-mats to make is one which uses any 12″ (30.5 cm) block of patchwork with strips of plain, contrasting material sewn to either end. These ends should be quilted in an appropriate pattern and colour of thread, to add a decorative note to your mat (Plates 6 and 8). For instance, a Nine Patch block made with five brown and white gingham squares and four plain brown squares with ends of the same brown material is particularly effective if the quilting pattern on the ends is done with white thread.

Materials Required for One Place-Mat Based on a 12" (30.5 cm) Block
Measurements include a ¼" (6 mm) seam allowance.

Material to make a finished 12" (30.5 cm) square block in your chosen design
Two rectangles, measuring 3½" x 12½" (8.9 cm x 31.8 cm), in contrasting plain broadcloth for the ends
One rectangle, measuring 12½" x 18½" (31.8 cm x 47 cm), of the same broadcloth for the back
One rectangle of quilt batting in the same size as the back rectangle

Sewing Instructions
Sew the patches for the patchwork block together and press well. The block should measure 12½" (31.8 cm) square. Sew the end strips of plain material to two opposite sides of the block allowing a ¼" (6 mm) seam allowance. Press the seams toward the ends. Trace on any needed quilting lines. Place the lining and patchwork top, right sides together, on top of the quilt batting. Pin the corners securely and match the sides carefully. Baste if necessary. Machine stitch, leaving a ¼" (6 mm) seam allowance around the outside edge of the mat, leaving an opening on one side for turning it right side out. Trim the batting if necessary. Turn the mat, carefully pulling out the corners and edges. Blind stitch the opening closed. Press edges very lightly with a steam iron — DO NOT FLATTEN. Baste the layers together as instructed for preparing blocks for quilting on a frame in Chapter 4, p. 28. Pin the place-mat on the frame and quilt as usual through all layers — the quilting stitches will show on the back.

FIELD OF DIAMONDS PLACE-MAT (Plate 6)
A very striking place-mat may be made with the hexagon pattern described in Grandmother's Flower Garden in Chapter 1, p. 15. When the hexagons are set together in this way it is called Field of Diamonds.

Materials Required for One Place-Mat
Using the hexagon pattern from Chapter 1, p. 15, cut 15 plain hexagons and 28 printed hexagons
One piece of lining material, measuring 18" x 20" (45.7 cm x 50.8 cm)
One piece of quilt batting the same size as the lining material

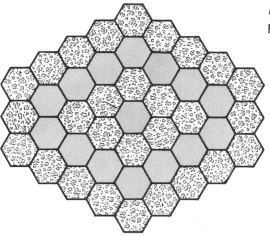

Fig. 25
Field of Diamonds

Sewing Instructions

Sew the first row of hexagons together around a plain centre hexagon
as directed for Grandmother's Flower Garden in Chapter 1, p. 16.
When the first circle is completed around the centre hexagon, sew the
two printed hexagons on opposite sides as shown in the diagram
above. Following the diagram, continue to sew the remaining two
rows. Press well. Place the patchwork block on top of the rectangular
lining piece, right sides together. Place both pieces on top of the
batting with the lining next to the batting. Pin the edge of the
hexagon top securely and baste if necessary. Machine stitch around
the outside of the hexagon top ¼" (6 mm) from the edge, leaving a
place open to turn the mat right side out. Cut the lining and batting
to its proper shape by following the edges of the hexagons and clip
almost to the stitching line at all angles. If the angles have been
properly clipped, the place-mat will lie flat when turned. Turn the
mat right side out and blind stitch the opening shut. Press the edge
lightly making sure all the points have been pulled out. The mat is
now ready to be basted for quilting on your frame. Follow the
directions in Chapter 4, p. 28, preparing a block for quilting on a
frame.

PLAIN PLACE-MATS WITH CONTRAST QUILTING

The sand and blue place-mats in Plate 6 present a more formal
appearance and lend themselves to fine table settings. Such place-
mats are particularly effective if made from a pastel colour and
quilted in a darker thread of the same shade. Let your imagination
really go to work in creating dainty patterns from flowers, leaves and
stems such as those shown on the mat in the picture. The place-mats

may be rectangular or oval, the latter having a finished size of approximately 12" x 20" (30.5 cm x 50.8 cm) or they may be wedge-shaped to fit a round table as illustrated by the blue mat in the picture and should measure approximately 13½" x 18½" (34.3 cm x 47 cm). Don't forget to add seam allowances to these measurements.

Sewing Instructions

After deciding on the shape and size of your place-mat, cut out a paper pattern which includes a ¼" (6 mm) seam allowance. Next, decide on a quilting pattern. Using your paper pattern as a guide, cut two pieces of broadcloth for the top and back and one piece of quilt batting. Trace your quilting pattern on the top piece. With right sides together, place the top and back on the batting. Machine stitch all around using a ¼" (6 mm) seam allowance, leaving an opening to turn the mat right side out. Trim the batting if necessary. Turn the mat right side out and blind stitch the opening closed. Press the edges very lightly — do not flatten. Baste for quilting and quilt on your frame as described in Chapter 4, p. 28.

Variations

A reversible place-mat may be made by simply making the front of plain fabric, quilted in a pleasing design, and the back of a figured contrast material. If you wish, your serviettes may then be made of the figured material.

See Chapter 9, p. 92, for Christmas place-mats.

SERVIETTES

To make serviettes I use one of the materials incorporated in the place-mat. Cut them 15" (38.1 cm) square for a luncheon size. Three serviettes can be cut from a 45" (1.14 m) width of material. Sew a very narrow rolled hem all around.

HOT MAT COVERS (Plate 7)

Why not complete your place-mat set with covers for some hot mats? Either square or round hot mats with asbestos backs and metal surfaces may be purchased very cheaply. The cover is made with a quilted block sewn to a back piece in pillowcase fashion allowing the mat to be slipped inside. The finished cover should be ¼" (6 mm) larger than the mat to allow for easy insertion.

Adapting Pattern Sizes for Hot Mat Covers

If you have never changed the size of a patchwork design, then start with something simple such as a basic four-patch block following these basic rules. Follow the instructions immediately following Crosses and Losses for the more difficult patterns and designs.

Crosses and Losses — a Basic Four Patch Block

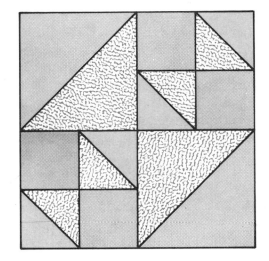

Fig. 26
Crosses and Losses

1. Draw a 7¼″ (18.4 cm) square (to fit the hot mat) on a piece of paper. Divide it into four equal quarters.
2. Following the above diagram, divide one quarter into four more quarters and repeat for the diagonally opposing square.
3. Now draw a diagonal line as shown across two of these small quarters. Repeat for the diagonally opposing corner.
4. In the two remaining large quarters draw a diagonal line across the square.

Your pattern is now complete. You will see this particular design has only three basic patch shapes — a large triangle, a small triangle and a small square. Cut these three pattern pieces from the square and trace onto cardboard to make the templates. Write the number of fabric pieces required on each template. Remember to add a ¼″ (6 mm) seam allowance when cutting the fabric.

You may adapt any basic 4, 9, 16 or 25-patch block in the same manner to any size square. Nine-patch blocks should first be divided into three equal sections in both directions across the square. This gives nine equal squares to draw in the required pattern lines. Sixteen and 25-patch designs are adapted by first dividing the square into 16 or 25 equal squares and then, following a diagram of the desired pattern, drawing in the necessary lines.

Materials Required for One Square Patchwork Hot Mat Cover

Materials required to sew one 7¼″ (18.4 cm) square finished patchwork block

One 7¾″ (19.7 cm) square of backing material for patchwork top
One 7¾″ (19.7 cm) square of quilt batting
One 7¾″ (19.7 cm) square of fabric for the back of the mat

Sewing Instructions

Sew the patchwork top together as usual and press. It should measure 7¾″ (19.7 cm) including the seam allowance. Place the top and square of the backing material, right sides together, on top of the quilt batting. Machine sew ¼″ (6 mm) from the edge across one side of the square through all layers. Turn the patchwork top back over the batting and backing material with the right side up. Lightly press the finished edge. DO NOT FLATTEN. Since the cover is sewn together in pillowcase fashion, this will be the finished edge for the opening. The top is now ready to be basted and quilted. Turn in a ¼″ (6 mm) hem on one side of the square for the back of the "pillowcase." Place the quilted block and the back, right sides together, with the finished edges on the same side. Pin, matching the raw edges and corners. Sew ¼″ (6 mm) from the edge on the three unfinished sides. Turn right side out and insert the hot mat.

Quilted Covers for Hot Mats to Fit Various Shapes

A pattern may be made for any hot mat by tracing around its outside edges. Add ¼″ (6 mm) all around to allow the cover to fit easily over the mat. If the mat itself is very thick then allow extra for this as well. It is better to have the cover a little too large than too small. Cut out three pieces of fabric ¼″ (6 mm) larger than the pattern — one for the surface, one for the backing of the quilted top and one for the back side of the mat cover. Cut a piece of batting the same size. Trace a quilting pattern on the top surface. Then sew as instructed for the preceding hot mat covers, being sure to leave a large enough opening on one side to insert the hot mat.

TABLE RUNNER AND HOT MAT COVERS IN OHIO STAR PATTERN (Plate 8)

Draft a pattern using a 7¼″ (18.4 cm) square for the Ohio Star design following the instructions as given in this chapter on "Adapting Pattern Sizes for Hot Mat Covers," and following the directions for adapting a basic nine-patch design.

The same pattern size used for the Ohio Star runner may be used to make the hot mat covers as directed in this chapter.

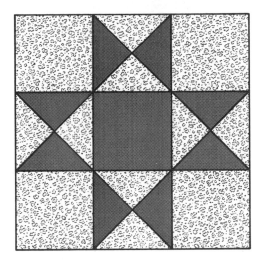

Fig. 27
Ohio Star

Sewing Instructions

Cut out the paper pattern pieces. There are only two shapes used — a triangle and a square. You will need two Ohio Star blocks for the runner. Trace the required number of pieces for each template onto the material. Remember to add a ¼″ (6 mm) seam allowance when cutting out the patches.

1. Sew the patches together for both blocks. Press.
2. Place the two blocks on the diagonal with corners meeting in the centre.
3. Cut out another 7¼″ (18.4 cm) square from paper. Draw a diagonal line from one corner to the opposite corner. Cut along this line. This large triangle will fit into either side of the blocks in the middle section of the runner.
4. Using this pattern, cut out two large fabric triangles remembering to add a ¼″ (6 mm) seam allowance when cutting.
5. Cut the remaining paper triangle in half and using this pattern and the same material as that for the large centre triangles, cut out four triangles. These smaller triangles fit at the four outside corners of the runner making it into a rectangle.
6. Following Fig. 28 sew one side of one large triangle to one side of one block. Sew the corner triangles onto the other sides of the block. Repeat this procedure for the other half of the runner and then sew one straight seam across the centre to join the halves together.
7. Cut one piece of quilt batting measuring 11″ x 21″ (28 cm x 53.3 cm) and a piece of backing material in the same size.
8. With right sides together, place the top and backing on top of the batting.

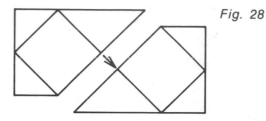

Fig. 28

9. Machine stitch all around ¼" (6 mm) from the edge, leaving an opening for turning on one side. Trim the batting if necessary and turn right side out. Blind stitch the opening closed. Press the edges lightly.
10. Baste for quilting and quilt on your frame as directed in Chapter 4, p. 28.

POT HOLDERS (Plate 11)

Pot holders can be made from the same small patchwork squares used for the hot mat covers. I machine sew the patches for pot holders reserving my hand sewing for those pieces where hand work will be appreciated. Pot holders or oven mitts should be made of 100% cotton materials because of their better capability to withstand heat. I use a double layer of polyester quilt batting for interlining. If you have any cotton quilt batting on hand you may prefer to use that but I find polyester batting quite satisfactory.

Materials Required for One Pot Holder

One completed patchwork top in a 7¼" (18.4 cm) square plus a seam allowance as described for hot mat covers
One 7¾" (19.7 cm) square of plain broadcloth for the back
Two 7¾" (19.7 cm) squares of quilt batting. If you use cotton batting one layer will probably be sufficient.

Sewing Instructions

Place the back and the patchwork front, right sides together, on top of the two pieces of quilt batting. Pin, matching all corners and raw edges. Sew around with ¼" (6 mm) from the edge leaving an opening through which to turn the pot holder right side out. Trim the batting if necessary. Turn right side out and blind stitch the opening closed. Gently press, pulling out the edges and corners well. Baste as for quilting a block. Quilt on your lap board. If you find it difficult to quilt through the double layer of batting then blind quilt it on the seam lines of the pattern where your stitches will be hidden.

OVEN MITTS (Plate 11)

This oven mitt has a separate cover over the padded mitt inside. Not only can the outside be easily removed for laundering but you may also make several different mitt covers including one of Christmas prints for the Christmas season. The materials used should be of 100% cotton for the outside but a double layer of polyester quilt batting works well for the padding. The quilted inside liner is made first and then the outside cover is made separately.

Materials Required to Make One Mit

Double the quantities to make a pair.

Liner — four pieces of quilt batting cut from the enlarged mitt pattern
— four mitt pieces of unbleached cotton or other cotton material
Outside — two pieces of calico ½″ (1.3 cm) larger all round than the mitt pattern
— bias tape to bind the wrist edge

Sewing Instructions

Enlarge the mitt pattern on paper ruled into 1″ (2.5 cm) squares.

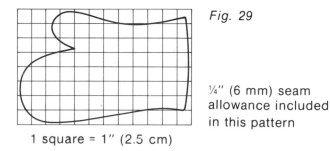

Fig. 29

¼″ (6 mm) seam allowance included in this pattern

1 square = 1″ (2.5 cm)

Liner

It is important to note that the seam allowance is included in this pattern. On opposite sides of two of the cotton mitt pieces (one for each side of the mitt liner) rule lines 1½″ (3.8 cm) apart in an all-over diamond pattern for quilting. For each side of the mitt liner place two pieces of quilt batting between two cotton mitt pieces using one plain piece and one with ruled lines. Pin and baste the layers together very well as the cotton tends to wander over the thick batting when it is quilted. You may quilt this by hand but it is easier to machine quilt it using a long stitch and a looser tension than usual. When both sides have been quilted sew them together using a ¼″ (6 mm) seam allowance stretching the seam slightly as you sew to flatten the material. Trim the batting back to the edge of the fabric. Either bind or zigzag around the wrist edge. Clip to the seam line between the thumb and palm of the mitt. Do not turn but leave the seam on the outside.

Outside Cover

Make the outside mitt ½″ (1.3 cm) larger all around to allow it to slip easily over the inside liner. Fold the calico material right sides together and cut one pair of mitt pieces in the larger size. With right sides together, sew around using a ¼″ (6 mm) seam allowance, leaving the wrist edge open. Clip almost to the seam line between the thumb and palm. Turn, press and bind around the wrist edge with bias tape making a loop for hanging at one of the seams. Insert the mitt liner inside the cover.

TEA AND COFFEE COSIES (Plate 9)

There is nothing nicer than a pretty cosy to keep tea piping hot. If tea should be hot so should coffee. If you have a china coffee pot or know someone who has, try making a coffee cosy as well. The simplest kind of tea or coffee cosy is a two-sided one and since pots come in all sizes they really need to be individually tailored for each pot.

To Make a Pattern for a Two-Sided Tea or Coffee Cosy

Measure the pot from the tip of its spout to the widest part of its handle allowing your tape to follow the widest curves of the side of the pot. Measure the height of the pot from the base, again allowing your tape to follow the curves of the pot to its highest point. Add 1½″ (3.8 cm) to the width and height measurements. This will allow for a ¼″ (6 mm) seam allowance. Now draw a rectangle on paper according to the length and width measurements. Curve or round the two top corners for a more pleasing appearance. Decide on a pattern for the outside. You may wish to use a pretty piece of printed fabric and quilt around the pattern on the fabric. If you wish to use squares or rectangles, simply divide the surface into the number of equal squares or rectangles you desire and round off the edges on the two top corners. You may also quilt on plain material or use appliqué.

Sewing Instructions

Both sides of the cosy should be quilted using a piece of quilt batting and a lining fabric the same size as the outside pieces. The lining fabric will be the lining for the inside of your cosy. When the sides are quilted, place them right sides together and sew the sides and top of the outside fabric using a ¼″ (6 mm) seam allowance, leaving the batting and lining free. Overlap the batting on itself. Turn in the ¼″

(6 mm) seam allowances toward each other on the two lining pieces. Blind stitch together. Turn the cosy right side out. Finish the bottom edge with a 1½″ (3.8 cm) wide piece of binding made from one of the fabrics used on the outside. Using a ¼″ (6 mm) seam allowance, this will make a ½″ (1.3 cm) binding all around. It is not necessary to cut this binding on the bias as it is being applied to a straight edge.

TOTE BAGS (Plate 5)
This handy bag with its fabric handle can be made from any two quilted blocks of patchwork or appliqué.

Materials Required for a Patchwork or Appliqué Bag
Two quilted blocks of patchwork or appliqué in your choice of pattern
One piece of lining material measuring the width of the block and twice the length
One strip of fabric for the handles, measuring 4″ x 32″ (10.1 cm x 81.2 cm)

Sewing Instructions
1. Complete two quilted blocks in the design and size of your choice.
2. With right sides together sew three sides of the blocks through all layers of material and batting. Turn right side out.
3. Fold the lining material in half and stitch using a ¼″ (6 mm) seam allowance on the two side seams. Leave the lining inside out. Slide the lining inside the bag, wrong sides together.
4. To make the handles turn in the raw edges along the length of the strip to meet in the centre. Fold in half again and, using your sewing machine, top stitch ¼″ (6 mm) from both edges with two or three more rows of stitching in between for strength. Cut in half thereby making two handles.
5. To finish the top edge of the bag, turn the edges of the quilted block and lining in ¼″ (6 mm) toward each other and pin together. Place the handles approximately 3½″ (8.9 cm) in from the sides and tuck down ½″ (1.3 cm) between the lining and blocks. Edge stitch all around the top.

CRAZY PATCHWORK TOTE BAG (Plate 5)
Frugal housewives used this method of quilt-making in order not to waste even a scrap of usable material from old clothing or household goods. By Victorian times crazy patchwork had become highly decorative as the fashions of that age dictated and were made of velvets, silks and satins and ornamented with elaborate embroidery. Heavier materials may also be used in this design such as wools, corduroys and knits.

Crazy patchwork requires a good eye in order to fit together, with balance, small pieces of material in varying shades and sizes. Experiment a little to begin with. Cut a piece of foundation material into the proper size for your project and then by shifting pieces of material around and cutting shapes and sizes you will soon find a pleasing arrangement. The method used here of placing all the pieces on the batting and sewing them all to a foundation piece produces a soft appearance and yet will give enough body to make excellent tote bags, tea and coffee cosies, shoe bags or appliance covers as well as the old-time quilts.

General Directions for Sewing Crazy Patchwork
If you wish to use quilt batting, cut the batting the same size as the foundation piece and lay it on top of the material. Starting in one corner of foundation material lay the patches on the batting, overlapping subsequent pieces by ½″ (1.3 cm). Turn under the edge, pin and continue until the foundation piece is covered. Baste the edges of the pieces down. Then sew along each patch with a small stitch through all layers. Embroider around each piece with an embroidery stitch of your choosing in whatever colour or colours seem appropriate. Part of this stitching should go over the seam and through the batting and foundation piece.

Materials Required for a Crazy Patchwork Tote Bag
Two pieces of foundation fabric, measuring 12½″ x 14½″ (31.8 cm x 36.8 cm)
Two pieces of quilt batting in the same size as the foundation fabric
One piece of lining material, measuring 12½″ x 28½″ (31.8 cm x 72.4 cm)
One strip of fabric for the handles, measuring 4″ x 32″ (10.1 cm x 81.2 cm)

Sewing Instructions
Lay the batting on top of one of the foundation pieces. Follow the general directions above for arranging and sewing the patches. Repeat for the second side. Trim the batting back to the edge of the foundation material if necessary. With right sides together, matching corners and sides, pin well making sure the patchwork is caught in a ¼″ (6 mm) seam allowance. To finish the bag follow the directions for the quilted tote bag in this chapter.

SHOE BAGS
One Christmas a few years ago I went to buy a shoe bag for my sister only to learn that they were not easily found and the bags I did find were not particularly attractive. That was when I decided to quilt my shoe bags from then on.

Fig. 30

The directions which follow use plain material with an ornately quilted pattern. Appliqué could also be used. The finished size measures 12″ (30.5 cm) wide and 14″ (35.5 cm) long. Refer to Chapter 6, p. 45, for Log Cabin bags.

QUILTED SHOE BAG

Materials Required
Two pieces of plain broadcloth, measuring 12½″ x 14½″ (31.8 cm x 36.8 cm)
Two pieces of pretty lining material the same size as the broadcloth
Two pieces of quilt batting the same size as the broadcloth
One 39″ (1 m) length of cording to close the top of the bag
One 26″ (66 cm) length of bias tape (same colour as the lining)

Sewing Instructions
Decide on a quilting pattern for the outside of the bag. I use dark broadcloth and quilt the pattern in light coloured thread. Since the top of the bag will be gathered together with a cord for closing, keep your quilting pattern on the lower two-thirds of the bag so it will show. Quilt both sides of the bag on your frame just as you would any block. Refer to Chapter 4, p. 28, for quilting directions.

1. Place the right sides of the quilted blocks together. Using a ¼″ (6 mm) seam, sew together only the outside surfaces on the two sides and across the bottom keeping the batting and lining free.

2. Overlap the batting on itself and turn the lining edges in ¼″ (6 mm) toward each other. Pin and blind stitch the seam around the three sides.
3. To finish the top edge, turn the outside and the lining edges in ¼″ (6 mm) toward each other and top stitch all around.
4. Work two small buttonholes through all layers 1¼″ (3.2 cm) from the top edge and approximately ½″ (1.3 cm) from either side of one of the side seams.
5. On the inside of the bag, centre the bias binding over the button-holes. Machine stitch close to both edges of the binding all around the bag making sure it is evenly spaced from the top edge of the bag. Overlap the ends of the binding. This forms the tunnel through which to thread the cording.
6. If the cording is too long after insertion cut off the ends. Put a knot in each end to prevent fraying. Then knot the two ends of the cording together approximately 2″ (5 cm) from these ends.

CRAZY PATCHWORK SHOE BAG

Materials Required
Two rectangles of crazy patchwork, measuring 12½″ x 14½″ (31.8 cm x 36.8 cm)
One piece of lining material, measuring 12½″ x 28½″ (31.8 cm x 72.4 cm)
One 39″ (1 m) length of cording for a draw-string

Sewing Instructions
Make up the two rectangles in crazy patchwork as directed for the crazy patchwork tote bag in this chapter and sew them together. Turn the bag right side out and, before inserting the lining, make two buttonholes through all layers, 1½″ (3.8 cm) from the top edge and ½″ (1.3 cm) from both sides of one of the side seams. Fold the lining material right sides together and sew the seams on both sides. Leave the lining material wrong side out and insert inside the crazy patch-work bag. Turn in top edges of the outside and the lining ¼″ (6 mm) toward each other and top stitch all around on your sewing machine. Make a second row of stitching around the bag 1″ (2.5 cm) from the top edge and through all layers of material including the lining. Make a third row of stitching in the same fashion ½″ (1.3 cm) below the second row so that the buttonholes are between these rows of stitching. This forms a tunnel through which to thread the cording. Insert the cording as directed for the quilted shoe bag, immediately above.

LAUNDRY BAGS (Plate 10)

What is more useful than a laundry bag to hang on your bedroom door and what child wouldn't love these Sunbonnet Sue or Overall Sam bags. Of course, any appliqué pattern may be used. Crazy Patchwork also lends itself very effectively for a laundry bag and can be quickly made if the patches are zigzagged on your sewing machine.

SUNBONNET SUE OR OVERALL SAM LAUNDRY BAGS

Materials Required

One 39" (1 m) length of 36" (91.4 cm) wide broadcloth for the bag. (I use unbleached cotton, washed and dried.)
One piece of quilt batting, measuring 13" x 18" (33 cm x 45.7 cm)
Material to make an appliqué pattern — see Chapter 3, p. 20 or 23
One 10" (25.4 cm) length of ¾" (1.9 cm) wide elastic
One 39" (1 m) length of cording for hanging
One 12½" (31.8 cm) long piece of wood dowling, ½" (1.3 cm) in diameter

Sewing Instructions

1. Mark out and cut the various pieces from the broadcloth as directed in Fig. 31.
2. Cut out and baste under the seam allowances for Sunbonnet Sue or Overall Sam as directed in Chapter 3, p. 23, for appliqué. Centre the pieces on the front section of the bag approximately 2½" (6.3 cm) from the bottom and appliqué as directed in Chapter 3, p. 19.
3. Place the appliquéd front over the batting and backing piece. Baste together as directed in Chapter 4, p. 28, for quilting any block. Quilt on your frame around "Sue" or "Sam," adding any further quilting as desired.
4. Cut 1½" (3.8 cm) from across the top of the batting and backing piece. DO NOT CUT THE FRONT PIECE.
5. Turn the top of the front under ¼" (6 mm) and then turn down 1" (2.5 cm) overlapping over the batting and backing. Baste along the edge of the seam and machine stitch straight across through all layers to form a casing for the elastic.
6. Insert the elastic and sew the ends even with both sides. This will slightly gather the front of the bag.
7. Sew the ends of the two side strips together to form the sides and bottom of the bag with a ¼" (6 mm) French seam as follows: with wrong sides of strips facing, sew together using a ¼" (6 mm) seam

Fig. 31 Layout for cutting laundry bag

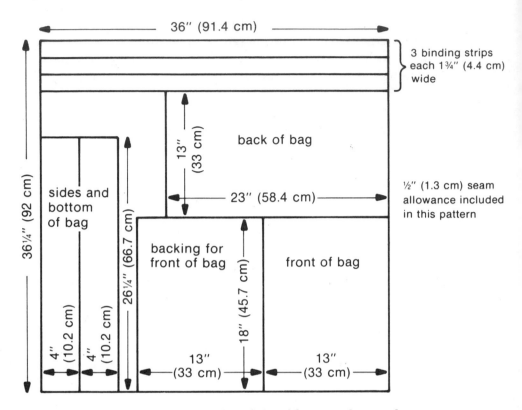

allowance. Turn the material right sides together and crease along the seam line. Stitch ¼″ (6 mm) from the fold. This is a French seam.

8. Turn both ends of this strip under ¼″ (6 mm) and then turn them down a further 1¼″ (3.1 cm). Sew and press.

9. With wrong sides together, pin the sides to the front, centring the French seam in the middle of the bottom. The seam allowance will be on the outside of the bag. This will be covered with the binding. Make sure all the layers of material are evenly lined up all the way around. Round the two bottom corners by trimming slightly. Baste. Do not sew together yet.

10. Sew the binding strips together in one long piece. Press open seams for less bulk. Press one side of the binding under ¼″ (6 mm).

11. With right sides of binding and front together, pin the unpressed raw edge of the binding strip to the front of the bag, matching the edges of the material as you work. Machine stitch using a ½″ (1.3 cm) seam allowance, rounding the two bottom corners. Turn

the binding over the seam onto the sides of the bag. Pin and hem down the ironed edge.

12. Turn down the top edge of the back bag piece 3¾" (9.5 cm) onto the back. Turn the edge under another ¼" (6 mm) and stitch straight across. This double layer adds strength to the top of the back of the bag for hanging.

13. Make another row of stitching 7/8" (2.2 cm) from the top edge to form a casing for the dowling. Do not insert the dowling yet.

14. Make a ½" (1.3 cm) buttonhole, 3½" (8.9 cm) from either side and just below the dowling casing, through which to thread the cording for the handle.

15. With the right side of the back against the wrong side of the sides and front, pin the back of the bag to the sides. The seam will be on the outside as for the front. The back will extend above the sides and front. Match the bottom centre and round the bottom corners. Baste.

16. Insert the dowling into the casing.

17. With right sides of the binding and sides together apply the binding over the seam as directed for the front, finishing by hand at either end of the dowling. Hem the binding down on the back side over the seam.

18. Insert the cording for hanging through the buttonholes and tie the ends around the dowling.

CRAZY PATCHWORK LAUNDRY BAG

Materials Required
One piece of unbleached cotton or other fabric, measuring 24" x 36" (61 cm x 91.4 cm), for the foundation
One 78" (2 m) length of cording for the top closing
A variety of fabrics for the patches

Sewing Instructions
1. There is no need to use batting in this bag. Simply arrange your patches in the desired shapes and colours over the entire surface of the rectangle in the same fashion as directed for the crazy patch-work tote bag in this chapter.

2. Stitch into place either by hand or machine, using embroidery if desired or zigzag each patch on your sewing machine.

3. After completing the crazy patchwork, fold the bag in half with right sides together so the bottom will measure 18" (45.7 cm) across. The fold will form one side of the bag. Sew up the other side and across the bottom.

4. Make four small buttonholes ¾" (1.9 cm) from the top edge, one on either side of the side seam and two more about ¾" (1.9 cm) apart on either side of the other side of the bag. These will be used to thread the cording through.
5. Turn down the top 2" (5 cm) on the inside and pin. Turn the raw edge under ¼" (6 mm) and stitch all round through all layers.
6. Make a second row of stitching 7/8" (2.2 cm) from top edge to form a casing for the cording.
7. Cut the cording in half. Thread one piece through a buttonhole into the casing and around the bag bringing the end out through the other buttonhole on the same side of the bag. The cording will form a "U," with only the two loose ends showing. Repeat with the second piece of cording starting with a buttonhole on the opposite side of the bag and running the cording around the bag. This will bring two ends out on each side of the bag.
8. Knot the two ends together at each side of the bag. Pull up the cording and hang the bag on your door knob.

WALL-HANGINGS

There was little room for the aesthetic in the harsh lives led by our pioneer ancestors but quilters found a real outlet in quilting for their artistic talents and their love of beauty. Wall-hangings are of ancient origin and although used at one time to warm the cold, stone walls of dwellings, their function is now purely artistic. If you cannot paint with a brush then use your creative talents to "paint" with a needle. Wall-hangings may be any size or shape which you desire. Basic directions for making them are much the same.

OVERALL SAM WALL-HANGING

Materials Required
Materials for Overall Sam appliqué — see Chapter 3, p. 23
One piece of broadcloth in a neutral colour for the background, measuring 11¾" x 17¾" (29.9 cm x 45.1 cm)
Two navy-coloured framing strips of broadcloth, measuring 3" x 16½" (7.6 cm x 41.9 cm)
Two navy-coloured framing strips of broadcloth, measuring 3" x 22½" (7.6 cm x 57.1 cm)
One piece of fabric for the back, measuring 16½" x 22¾" (41.9 cm x 60.3 cm)
One piece of quilt batting, measuring 16½" x 22½" (41.9 cm x 57.1 cm)

Plate 1. The key to success in lap quilting is the use of a tapestry frame on which to quilt the blocks. The side dowels may be turned to adjust for tension and size of block, thus ensuring ease of quilting and a smooth and square piece of work.

Plate 2. Appliquéd Grandmother's Flower Garden Quilt. The mosaic pattern is of old English upper-class origin, typical of the 1700s and 1800s.

(Opposite) Plate 3. Patchwork and appliquéd pillows with quilted backs.

(Above) Plate 4. Sunshine and Shadow log cabin quilt.

Plate 5.   Crazy Patchwork and Nine Patch tote bags; Log Cabin shoe bag and tote bags with wooden handles.

Plate 6.   Quilted and patchwork place-mats including Log Cabin and Field of Diamonds patterns, and appliquéd and patchwork Christmas mats.

Plate 7.   Hot mat covers in miniature patterns with metal hot-pad inserts.

Plate 8.   Ohio Star place-mat with centre runner and hot mat covers.

Plate 9.   Tea and coffee cosies with matching hot mat cover.

Plate 10.   Overall Sam, Sunbonnet Sue and Crazy Patchwork laundry bags.

Plate 11.   Patchwork pot holders and oven mitts with separate quilted insert.

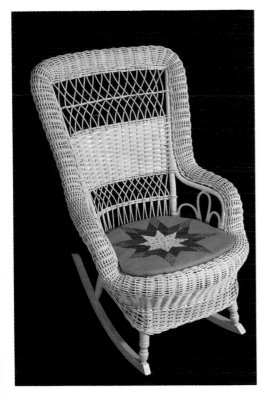

Plate 12.   Appliquéd Blazing Star chair pad.

Plate 13.   Patchwork and tufted chair pad with frill.

Plate 14.   Quilted book cover, jewellery or cosmetic bag, eyeglass case.

Plate 15.   Calico and appliquéd Christmas ornaments, wall-hanging, coasters and guest towels.

One 18" (45.7 cm) long piece of wood dowling ½" (1.3 cm) in diameter
One 24" (61 cm) length of cording for hanging

Fig. 32
What little boy wouldn't love Overall Sam hanging on his wall? Try using Sunbonnet Sue for a little girl's room.

Sewing Instructions

1. Cut out the fabric pieces for Overall Sam.
2. Centre the pattern and appliqué to the background material. Follow the directions for general appliqué as given in Chapter 3, p. 19. Add any embroidery as desired.
3. Sew on the framing strips using a ¼" (6 mm) seam allowance, mitring the corners. Press well.
4. Place the front, right side up, on a flat surface. Turn under the top edge of the frame ¼" (6 mm) and pin.
5. Lay the backing material, wrong side up, on top matching the bottom corners and side seams. The back piece will extend 1¼" (3.2 cm) beyond the top edge of the front. Pin.
6. Place the batting on top matching the edges with the front piece edges.

7. Machine stitch down each side and across the bottom. Do not sew across the top edge of the front.
   Turn right side out.
8. Pin the turned-under edge of the top front to the backing across the top 1¼″ (3.2 cm) from the raw edge, and hem down onto the backing material.
9. Turn down the backing 1¼″ (3.2 cm) onto the back of the hanging. None of the backing material should show above the top edge of the frame on the front. Turn under the raw edge ¼″ (6 mm) and hem across, making sure the stitches do not come through to show on the front. This is the tunnel for the dowling. Do not insert the dowling until the quilting is complete. Lightly press the edges.
10. Baste the hanging as directed in Chapter 4, "Assembling a Block for Quilting on a Lap Frame," p. 28, and quilt as directed on p. 29. The quilting stitches will show on the back of the hanging.
11. Insert the dowling and tie the cord to each end. Hang up your wall hanging.

See the directions in Chapter 9, p. 94, for a Christmas wall-hanging.

CHAIR PADS (Plates 12 and 13)

Since the size and shape of chair seats vary widely it is best to tailor a chair pad for the seat on which it is to be used. The easiest method is to make a paper pattern of the seat taking into account whether the pad is to come to the edge of the seat or whether a ruffle is to be used. If the pad is to be stuffed with polyester fibrefill it should be filled quite full for it will flatten considerably with sitting. This filling will take up extra material so allow a little extra in your measurements.

After making the pattern decide whether you wish to use patchwork, appliqué, or a tufted (tied) one-piece cover.

PATCHWORK PAD

After making the paper pattern divide it into a pleasing number of squares. Cut out one square as a pattern. Cut out the required number of squares to make the top of the pad, allowing a ½″ (1.3 cm) seam allowance. Machine stitch the squares together in strips before sewing the strips together. Place the paper pattern on top and shape the outside edges of the patchwork top if necessary. Plain broadcloth, in one of the colours used in the cover, may be used for the ties, frills and under-side of the pad. Read the directions in the next section for the ties and frill. After the pad is sewn together and stuffed, tie the pad with strong thread or synthetic wool through all layers at the intersections of the squares.

Sewing Pad Ties and Frill

For a strong tie, use a 2″ (5 cm) wide strip of fabric. Turn the edges to meet in the middle and fold in half to make a finished ½″ (1.3 cm) wide tie. Machine stitch. These will be sewn in at each back corner.

Since a frill will be sewn to only three sides, the length of the frill will be double the distance around the two sides and across the front of the pad. Sew the top, frill and backing together as described in Chapter 5, "To Make a Pillow with a Frill," p. 31, including the two back corner ties and leaving an opening for stuffing at the back. After the pad is stuffed, the opening is slip stitched closed.

EYEGLASS CASE (Plate 14)
Finished size: 3¼″ x 7″ (8.2 cm x 17.8 cm)

Materials Required
Two pieces of fabric for the outside, measuring 3¾″ x 7½″ (9.5 cm x 19.1 cm)
Two pieces of quilt batting the same size
Two pieces of lining material the same size

Sewing Instructions
Trace the quilting pattern on both outside pieces. Place one piece of batting on the wrong side of a lining piece. Lay the outside piece, right side up, on top. Pin, matching the raw edges of the three layers. Baste in a zigzag fashion through all three layers. Quilt with a contrasting colour of thread. Repeat for the second side. With right sides together, pin only the batting and outside surfaces together, matching the raw edges, leaving the lining free. Sew around the case through only the outside fabric and the batting using a ¼″ (6 mm) seam allowance, leaving an opening at the top above the quilted pattern. Trim back the batting if necessary. Turn in edges of the lining pieces ¼″ (6 mm) toward each other and blind stitch all around on the three sides. Turn the case right side out. Turn in the top edges of the lining and outside pieces ¼″ (6 mm) toward each other. Blind stitch around the top.

Fig. 33
Eyeglass Case

JEWELLERY OR COSMETIC BAG (Plate 14)
Finished size: 5" x 6½" (12.6 cm x 16.5 cm)

Materials Required
One piece of fabric for the outside, measuring 11" x 7" (28 cm x 17.7 cm)
One piece of lining material, measuring 10½" x 7" (26.7 cm x 17.7 cm)
One piece of quilt batting, measuring 10½" x 7" (26.7 cm x 17.7 cm)
One 6" (15.2 cm) zipper the same colour as the outside fabric

Sewing Instructions

The fabric rectangle for the outside will be folded in half with the fold line forming the bottom of the bag. In order to ensure that the quilting design appears in an upright position on both sides of the bag, centre the pattern (Fig. 34) with the top of the design about 1″ (2.5 cm) from one of the ends. Turn the pattern around 180° and follow the same procedure.

Lay the batting on top of the wrong side of the lining piece. Centre the outside piece, right side up, on top of the batting and lining. There will be a ¼″ (6 mm) overhang beyond the lining edge at both ends. Match and pin together the long edges of all layers. With a basting stitch, zigzag all three layers together to hold them in place for quilting. Quilt the designs with a contrasting colour of thread. Fold the bag in half, right sides together, with a quilted design on each half. Match the raw edges. Fold the lining back on each side and sew the outside cover and the batting leaving a ¼″ (6 mm) seam allowance, from the top of the bag to the bottom. Trim back the batting if necessary. Turn in the lining edges ¼″ (6 mm) toward each

Fig. 34
Jewellery or
Cosmetic Bag

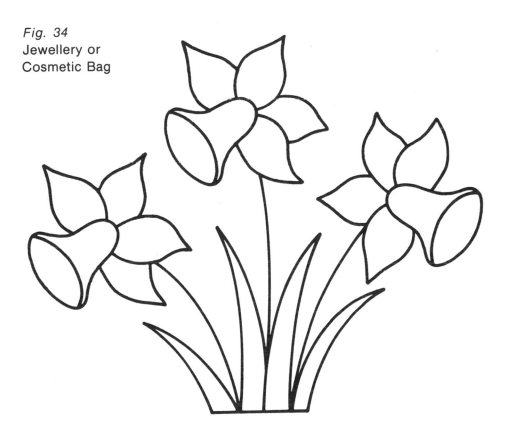

other and blind stitch together. Turn the bag right side out. Turn down the outside top edge ¼" (6 mm) on the inside over the batting and lining. Baste all around. Fit the zipper in between the basted edges and hand sew through the zipper tapes allowing the two edges of the bag to meet in the middle of the zipper.

BOOK COVER (Plate 14)

Since books vary widely in size and thickness the general directions which I have given below may be followed to make a quilted cover for any book. A quilting design suitable to the cover size would have to be used. The pattern shown is designed to fit a closed book, measuring 5¾" x 8½" (14.6 cm x 21.5 cm).

Sewing Instructions

The width of the finished cover should be ¼" (6 mm) wider than the book. Wrap the fabric around the closed book in the same manner as a paper jacket, folding each end flap inside the book cover 3¼" (8.2 cm). This will be the length of your finished cover. Then add on a ¼" (6 mm) seam allowance all around. Cut a piece each of lining and quilt batting the same size as the covering fabric. With the fabric wrapped around the book, mark the area for the quilting pattern on the front with pins. Trace on a design of your choice. On the back fabric cover draw straight lines for quilting equidistant from all edges of the closed book forming a rectangle. This will help to hold the batting in place. Lay the lining and outside pieces right sides together on top of the batting. Leaving an opening at one end for turning the cover right side out, machine stitch around the edges of the cover leaving a ¼" (6 mm) seam allowance. Trim back the batting and clip the corners. Turn right side out. Blind stitch the opening closed. Baste around the outside edges and press lightly. Baste the cover for quilting as directed for quilt blocks in Chapter 4, p. 28. Pin on your tapestry frame and quilt the design. Remove the basting threads. Wrap the cover around the book centring the front design on the front cover. Turn in the fabric flaps, pin and slip stitch in place at the top and bottom edges of the cover.

Fig. 35
Book Cover

8 Sewing A Quilt With Lap Quilted Blocks

STEPS IN PLANNING A QUILT
You would like to make a quilt but you just don't have the space in your home to set up a large frame. Then lap quilting is your answer. Both the Grandmother's Flower Garden quilt (Plate 2) and the Log Cabin quilt (Plate 4) were made in my lap in spare moments while meals were cooking, while I was chatting with a friend or at the cottage on holiday.

Quilts should be well planned before beginning the work. Read this chapter carefully before starting. Follow the steps below and you will have no problems in making a beautiful lap-quilted quilt. (To plan and sew a Log Cabin quilt see the directions in Chapter 6, p. 33.)

A Quilt Or a Coverlet?
Decide whether you want a quilt to act as a blanket only or a coverlet covering the pillows and used with or without a dust ruffle. A coverlet will be larger than a quilt used only as a blanket and will involve more work and material.

Size
Decide on the size of your coverlet or quilt. Since bed measurements vary in length, width and height it is best to measure the bed for which you intend the coverlet or quilt. The general rules given below are based on a double bed, measuring 6' (1.8 m) long and 54" (1.4 m) wide and a single bed measuring 6' (1.8 m) long and 39" (1 m) wide.

COVERLET
DOUBLE BED The coverlet should measure 108" (2.7 m) long, if you wish it to cover the pillows, and at least 84" (2.1 m) wide depending on

72

how far down you wish the coverlet to hang and whether you plan to
use a dust ruffle.

SINGLE BED The coverlet should be the same length as for a double
bed and measure at least 72″ (1.8 m) wide again depending on how
far down you wish it to hang.

QUILT

DOUBLE BED Measure the length of the mattress and add on its depth.
Add a further 12″ (30.5 cm) to permit tucking in the finished quilt
when you are making up the bed. Many quilters prefer a length
somewhere between 100″ (2.5 m) and 108″ (2.7 m) with a minimum
of 90″ (2.3 m). The absolute minimum width is 72″ (1.8 m) but 84″
(2.1 m) is generally preferred but measure to be sure. Don't forget
that people sleep in beds and take up part of the width!

SINGLE BED Measure the length as directed for a double bed immediately
above. Then measure the width using 68″ (1.7 m) as a minimum.

Decide on the "Set" of Your Quilt

The manner in which finished blocks are set together is of utmost
importance to the final appearance of the quilt. Take any design and
the appearance will be completely changed by sewing block to block,
using dark or light lattice strips, or alternating ornately quilted,
solid-coloured blocks. Decide whether you wish to use a border and
its width. The size of the block may have to be altered (refer to
Chapter 7, p. 51) depending on your needs or it may be necessary to
vary the width of the lattice strips to achieve the required size. You
individualize your quilt.

THE BLOCKS

Some blocks must be joined block to block for overall effect, i.e., Rob
Peter to Pay Paul, or Log Cabin.

If you wish each block to retain its identity then separate all your
blocks by lattice strips or ornately quilted blocks. The latter method
is very popular as it allows designs to stand out boldly.

Some blocks with a decided top and bottom such as Noon Day Lily
are best set on an angle with alternating quilted blocks and finished
with quilted triangles fitting in at the sides of the quilt.

LATTICE WORK

Lattice work (strips or sash work) is the next most popular set. The
finished lattice is usually 3″ to 4″ (7.5 cm to 10 cm) wide plus a
¼″ (6 mm) seam allowance. If the lattice is the same colour as the

background of the block then it serves to space the blocks. If a contrasting colour is used then it acts as a frame for each block which becomes more prominent.

Lattices may be made of one continuous piece of either printed or plain fabric, or may be made with pieced squares at the corners of each of the blocks. The squares at these intersections may be in a contrasting colour. Some quilters believe "intersections" should be used even if made in the same colour as the rest of the lattice because it helps assure the horizontal and vertical alignment of the blocks. (See Figs. 36 and 37.)

BORDERS

In earlier years patchwork quilts were usually finished with binding while the more elaborate appliqué quilts were often finished with an ornate border. Today, borders are used or not used according to the wishes of the quilter.

Borders vary as widely as do people since the border on your quilt will reflect you. A border acts as a frame for your quilt and without it some quilts may look like unframed pictures. I like to sew the blocks together, completing the main part of the quilt, before I finally decide on my border design. Just as it is hard to choose a picture frame without the picture, it is equally hard to choose a border without the sewn blocks. Try various designs by draping samples of material along the sides. There are not set rules for border designs but a few basic techniques may help you make your decision.

The easiest border is one which is either equal all around or narrower at the sides and wider at the ends. With the latter arrangement, corners cannot be mitred. The border may be made from the same colour of fabric used in the background of the block or the colour of the lattices, if used, beautifully quilted and bound around the edges. The quilting pattern should complement and not overpower the design of the blocks. If lattices are not used and the border is of the same colour as the background of the blocks, then it may be bound in a colour repeated from the quilt design.

A very effective border may be made of two or three coloured bands, either equal in width or in varying widths, and in colours picked up from the quilt blocks (Plate 4). Such a border may be blind quilted along the seam lines of the bands.

A wider border may be made with a patchwork or appliquéd design, or some part of the design used in the blocks may be repeated in the border corners. Patchwork borders are best used with patchwork quilts and, similarly, appliquéd borders are best on appliquéd quilts. The design must be kept simple so as not to overpower the centre of the quilt. Remember, the border is a frame. If the outer edge of the border is gently curved, let your design follow the curve. If appliquéd running vines are used, then the stems must be made from bias strips of material or purchased bias binding may be used.

BINDINGS
The binding encases the raw edges and adds the finishing touch to your quilt. A self-binding may be used where either the top or the back border piece is cut wider and brought over to the reverse side and hand stitched in place. This is the quickest method. A separate binding may also be used which will allow for a change should it begin to wear.

Designing the Quilt
On graph paper draw to scale the design for the entire quilt which you have decided upon, including lattice strips if used and the border. I find that it is a good idea to colour in at least part of the blocks to get a good idea of how the finished quilt will look.

Make the templates for the chosen quilt pattern and sew together one trial block to make sure all the patches fit properly. This will also help you to decide on your final colour scheme. Choosing fabric colours should be done carefully. I often try several colour schemes before deciding on a final one.

Estimating Yardage

BLOCKS
There are two methods for estimating yardage for the blocks:
1. Estimate how much yardage of each colour is needed for one block. Multiply by the number of blocks needed. Don't forget the lining for each block as well. This will be the lining for your quilt so use fabric that will compliment the top.
or
2. Add up the total number of fabric pieces required for each template for the finished quilt. Then calculate the yardage in each colour for that number of templates. Again don't forget the lining.

If ornately quilted alternating blocks are used remember to estimate the yardage for both the top and lining materials.

YARDAGE FOR LATTICE STRIPS, BORDERS AND BINDINGS

Borders and lattice strips may be made in one piece, cut lengthwise from the material or they may be pieced at the mid-point. Calculate the required yardage for the surface fabric and allow the same amount for the lining material.

When estimating yardage for bindings do not plan on cutting them on the bias unless they are to be sewn on a curved edge.

HOW MUCH QUILT BATTING?

For every top piece of the quilt you will require a piece of batting in the same size. One purchased quilt batt is usually enough to make a quilt for a double bed.

TO SEW TOGETHER A LAP QUILTED QUILT

The Blocks

Sew and quilt the number of blocks required for the quilt following the directions in Chapter 4, pp. 28 and 29. After all the blocks have been completed lay them out in their proper order. Following the steps below, sew them together to make strips across the width rather than lengthwise strips, since the shorter strips are easier to handle.

1. Place two blocks right sides together.
2. Fold back the batting and lining on each block and pin only the two top surfaces together, matching both corners first and then easing in the material if necessary.
3. Sew only the top surfaces together with a small running stitch ¼" (6 mm) from the edge, being careful not to catch the batting or lining.
4. Open the two blocks out flat, right sides down, on a hard surface (your lap board). Flatten the seam with your finger. Overlap the quilt batting over the seam by approximately ¼" (6 mm). Trim if necessary.
5. Overlap the two lining pieces and turn the top edge under ¼" (6 mm). Pin well. Do not overlap the lining more than the ¼" (6 mm) allowed or the top surface will tend to buckle.
6. Blind stitch the lining seam allowing your needle to penetrate into the layers of batting. This helps to hold the edges of the batting in place.
7. Continue sewing the blocks together in strips in the same manner. Each strip of blocks is then sewn to the next strip in exactly the same fashion, carefully matching the corners of the blocks.

Cutting Lattice Strips Without Intersections

If lattice work is to be used then a short strip will be sewn between each block in each row and a long strip will separate each row (Fig. 36).

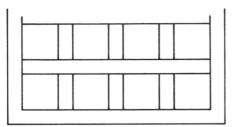

Fig. 36
Lattice strips between blocks and around outside of quilt

The short strips should be cut the length of one block and the desired width. After they are quilted (directions below) they will be sewn between each quilted block in the row. Long lattice strips to be sewn between the rows of blocks should be cut to run across the quilt as shown in Fig. 36. If the fabric for the lattice work is to be joined at a midway point, the seam should be sewn on the machine and pressed open to make it as inconspicuous as possible.

If lattice strips are to be used instead of a border around the outside edge of the quilt, leave these to add until after the blocks and lattices for the centre of the quilt are sewn together. They should be cut from long strips of fabric running the length and width of the outside edges or they may be joined at a midway point on the machine with the seam pressed open. Remember that for every piece of lattice you will need a piece of batting and a lining of the same size.

Cutting Lattice Strips with Intersections

If intersections are used, you must be very accurate with the seam allowances so that all blocks and intersections line up. Lattice strips with intersections are made by sewing one strip of lattice, which is the width of one block, to one square, which is the width of the lattice. Continue in this manner until you have reached the length of your cross-wise strip of blocks.

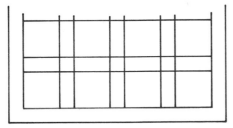

Fig. 37
Lattice strips with intersections between blocks

Cut each strip of lining and batting the finished length of each lattice strip. It is best to use a lattice border without intersections due to its superior strength.

Quilting Lattice Strips

Both long and short lattice strips are quilted in the following manner. Mark any quilting design on the top of the lattice strip before basting it together in a zigzag fashion with the batting and the lining. Make sure that the quilting lines come no closer than ½″ (1.3 cm) from the edge of the strip in order to allow seam allowances. Pin the strip on your tapestry frame and quilt as usual.

Sewing Lattice Strips Between the Blocks and Rows

The short lattice strips will be sewn between the blocks in each row and the long strips will be sewn between the completed rows running the width of the quilt. Make sure the blocks line up lengthwise of the quilt as you sew the rows to the lattices. The lattices are sewn on in exactly the same manner as used for sewing quilt blocks together. If intersections are used, make sure that all seams line up.

Borders

If the border fabric is to be joined at a midway point rather than cut from one strip of fabric it should be machine sewn and the seam pressed open to make it as inconspicuous as possible. Usually the corners of the border present a more pleasing appearance if they are mitred. One exception is the Log Cabin quilt where the square log design is better carried out in the border as well. This is also true for other quilts with similar designs.

After the blocks are sewn together for the centre of the quilt there are two methods of applying the border. If a straight border is being used then it may be quilted on your tapestry frame just as lattice strips are quilted, and then sewn onto the finished centre of the quilt in the same fashion used to sew blocks together.

The second method, and the one which I prefer, is to sew the border fabric onto the completed centre of the quilt and then quilt it

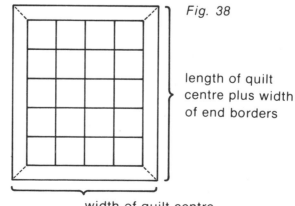

Fig. 38

length of quilt centre plus width of end borders

width of quilt centre plus width of side borders

with a quilting hoop as directed below. This ensures that your border will fit exactly.

1. Measure the length of the completed centre section of the quilt and add on double the width of the end border plus a little extra for safety.
2. Now measure the width of the completed quilt centre and add on double the width of the side border plus a little extra for safety.
3. Cut the border strips. Cut the lining material and quilt batting the same size.
4. With right sides together, pin the surface fabric of the border to the quilt. With right sides together, pin the lining on the back of the quilt. Pin the batting on top of the lining.
5. Sew through all layers to within ¼″ (6 mm) of each corner using with a ¼″ (6 mm) seam allowance. I machine stitch this for strength using a longer stitch than usual and less tension for a softer seam.
6. Continue in the same manner for all sides.
7. Mitre all the corners on the top fabric first and then the lining. Press the seams open. Trim the batting to just overlap at the corners.
8. Spread the quilt on a hard surface, right side up. Fold back the lining and batting under the quilt so the top border piece is smooth and flat with its right side up.
9. Trace on the quilting design. Then fold out the lining and batting matching the raw edges. Pin all the layers together and baste securely in a zigzag fashion.
10. Quilt using your quilting hoop.

Bindings

If a self-binding is used then the top border piece will need to be cut wider than the batting and lining to allow it to be turned over onto the back and hemmed down. If a separate binding is used, such a binding does not need to be cut on the bias unless a curved edge is to be bound. If the binding is cut on the straight of the grain, the seams where it is pieced in length should be matched, sewn on the bias, and pressed open. A finished binding should be ¾″ to 1″ (1.9 cm to 2.5 cm) wide. Add a ¼″ (6 mm) seam allowance to both raw edges and if the quilt batting is very thick a little extra may be allowed for this. I prefer to either hand sew or machine stitch the binding to the top side of the quilt and hem it down on the back side. If the corners of the border are mitred then also mitre the corners of the binding.

9 Christmas Calicos

Christmas begins on December 1st in our house. When our children were small we began the practice of bringing out one Christmas decoration each day, starting on the first day of December, as an outlet for their excitement. Although our children are now grown up we still continue this practice. In this way our house gradually becomes decorated and we are able to enjoy our Christmas ornaments over a longer period of time.

In this chapter I am including some Christmas decorations made from calicos and Christmas prints which I think you will enjoy making for your home or as gifts for friends and relatives. They are also good items to sell at bazaars.

CHRISTMAS TREE ORNAMENTS (Plate 15)
We have a small artificial Christmas tree which is just the right size to sit on top of a table. Before leaving for Florida in our house trailer one Christmas season we decided we really had to have a decorated Christmas tree so I made up calico ornaments to hang on our small tree. We all enjoyed our "old-fashioned" Christmas tree and we still continue to use it in our home each year. Such a tree makes a lovely gift for a person who cannot manage a tree for themselves. Packing is not a problem since nothing is breakable.

Sewing Instructions for Ornaments
Ornaments can be simply made from two pieces of material sewn together with an opening left for turning and stuffing with polyester fibrefill or old nylons. After blind stitching the opening closed add whatever decoration you wish. Let your imagination take over: the

Fig. 39 CHRISTMAS TREE ORNAMENTS
Cut 2 of each pattern. Add ¼″ (6 mm) seam allowance.

fabric used may be left plain; you might wish to use a piece of eyelette embroidery over this with the colour peeking through; you may use a green or red calico or small Christmas print. Bits of lace or rickrack may be added for decoration by slip stitching it to the finished edge. A pom-pom (use the balls from ball fringe) serves as a good clapper for a bell. Attach a hanger made from heavy thread or wool to slip over the branch of the tree at the top of the ornament. For more patterns use Christmas cookie cutters as guides and sew them in the same manner. Remember to add ¼″ (6 mm) seam allowance to the patterns.

CHRISTMAS GIFT BOX ORNAMENT   (Plate 15)

These little boxes with their cheery bows may be made in any size. A 2″ (5 cm) square box hangs nicely on the tree for an ornament. Larger ones may be made and set under a small table-top tree. They can be quickly put together on the sewing machine.

Materials Required for a 4″ (10 cm) Square Box

Six 4½″ (11.5 cm) squares for top, bottom and sides
Polyester fibrefill for stuffing
Bias binding or ribbon for tying up the box

Sewing Instructions

With right sides together, sew four of the squares in a row using a ¼″ (6 mm) seam allowance. Join the two ends. Fit one square into the top, matching the corners with the side seams. Sew around. Fit the bottom square into the box in the same fashion, leaving an opening on one side for turning and stuffing. Stuff fairly firmly, poking the fibrefill well out into the corners and keeping the sides as flat as possible. Blind stitch the opening closed. Using bias binding or a ribbon, tie around the box with a bow at the top.

CALICO CHRISTMAS TREE   (Plate 15)

Here is a tree that may be used for a wall-hanging but I prefer to put away some of my regular pillows which are around the house and replace them with a few of these. They add a bright and cheery note to any room.

Materials Required for One Tree

Ten red triangles and six green triangles cut from a variety of calicos
One piece of red or green broadcloth, measuring 18″ x 24″ (45.7 cm x
*   61 cm), for cutting the back of the tree and the front of the trunk*
Four white shirt buttons

Red or green ribbon for four small bows on the front
Polyester fibrefill for stuffing

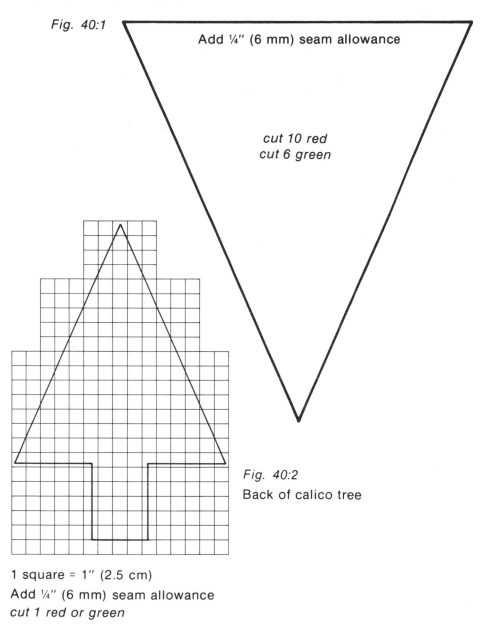

Fig. 40:1

Add ¼" (6 mm) seam allowance

cut 10 red
cut 6 green

Fig. 40:2
Back of calico tree

1 square = 1" (2.5 cm)
Add ¼" (6 mm) seam allowance
cut 1 red or green

Sewing Instructions

On paper ruled in 1" (2.5 cm) squares, enlarge the pattern for the back of the tree to scale. The triangle pattern for the front is full size and does not need enlarging. The finished size of the tree should measure approximately 15″ (38.1 cm) across the bottom of the tree and 22″ (56 cm) from the tip to the bottom of the trunk. Cut a rectangle, measuring 4¼″ x 5¾″ (10.8 cm x 14.6 cm), for the front of the trunk of the same material used for the back of the tree. This includes the seam allowance. Cut out the required number of triangles and the back piece adding a ¼″ (6 mm) seam allowance.

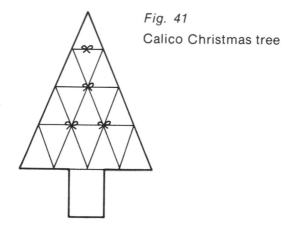

Fig. 41

Calico Christmas tree

Following the diagram and starting with a red triangle, machine stitch the triangles together in strips, across the width of the tree alternating the red and green colours. Then sew the strips together carefully matching the intersections of the triangles. Centre the front piece for the trunk on the base of the tree, and with right sides together, machine stitch using a ¼″ (6 mm) seam allowance. Press the seams well. With right sides together, sew the calico front to the plain back leaving an opening on one side for turning and stuffing. Clip the fabric on both sides of the trunk almost to the seam line at the point where it joins the body of the tree. Turn and stuff fairly firmly. Blind stitch the opening closed. Make four ribbon bows and sew them on as follows. Place a ribbon where indicated on Fig. 41 and match it with a button on the back of the tree. Sew the two together, drawing your thread through all layers of material and stuffing. The buttons prevent the stitches holding the ribbon from pulling through the material. Use strong thread and pull it through firmly, making a fairly deep indentation on the front. If you wish to hang the tree add a ribbon hanger on the top at the back.

CRAZY PATCHWORK CHRISTMAS STOCKING   (Plate 15)
This stocking will please the young at heart of all ages, from preschoolers right through to grandfather. In our home on Christmas morning these stockings are miraculously filled with all manner

of good things and usually with some favourite foods that are a little expensive for day-to-day eating but a real treat from Santa Claus.

Materials Required for One Stocking

A variety of materials from which to cut patches
One piece of foundation material, measuring 20″ x 28″ (51 cm x 71 cm), from which to cut the leg of the stocking and the backing for two toe pieces
One piece of red broadcloth, measuring 14″ x 25″ (35.5 cm x 63.5 cm), from which to cut the cuff and two toe pieces
One piece of quilt batting, measuring 14″ x 17″ (35.5 cm x 43.2 cm), for the cuff and two toe pieces
One 17″ (43.2 cm) length of ruffled lace or eyelette embroidery trim for around the cuff
Embroidery thread for decorative stitching

Fig. 42

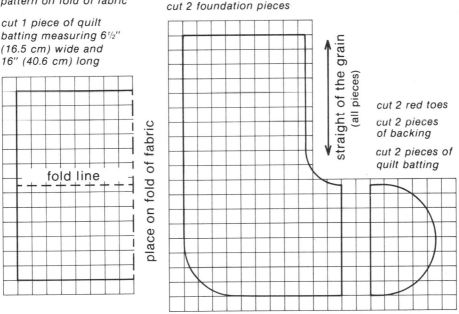

cut 1 red piece from pattern on fold of fabric

cut 1 piece of quilt batting measuring 6½″ (16.5 cm) wide and 16″ (40.6 cm) long

cut 2 foundation pieces

straight of the grain (all pieces)

cut 2 red toes

cut 2 pieces of backing

cut 2 pieces of quilt batting

fold line

place on fold of fabric

1 square = 1″ (2.5 cm)
½″ (1.3 cm) seam allowance included in this pattern

Sewing Instructions

Enlarge the pattern pieces to scale on paper ruled in 1″ (2.5 cm) squares. A ½″ (1.3 cm) seam allowance is included in the pattern. The length of the pattern for the stocking leg without the cuff should measure approximately 18″ (46 cm).

1. Cut out the stocking pieces as directed.
2. Lay out the patches on the foundation pieces for the leg. For directions for placing the patches refer to "Crazy Patchwork Tote Bag," p. 51. Do not use batting in the leg. Baste the overlapping patches. It is not necessary to sew each patch to the foundation as it is in a bag or a quilt. The embroidery stitches which should overlap each seam will hold the pieces in place. A feather stitch done with three strands of embroidery thread is quick and easy as well as decorative.
3. Trace all-over diamond quilting lines on the red toe pieces. Place one red toe piece and the batting on top of its backing piece. Baste together and quilt on your lap board. Repeat for the other side of the toe.
4. With right sides together, machine stitch one toe piece to one leg piece ½″ (1.3 cm) from the edge. Repeat for the other side of the stocking.
5. Place the stocking pieces right sides together and, starting at the top, sew ½″ (1.3 cm) from the edge all around the stocking leaving the top open. Turn the stocking right side out.
6. Fold the cuff piece in half along the fold line. Trace on a quilting pattern to cover the cuff to within ½″ (1.3 cm) of either end.

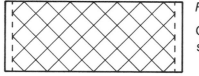

Fig. 43

Quilting pattern for stocking cuff

7. Place the quilt batting inside the folded cuff, baste and quilt on your frame. Remove basting threads.
8. With right sides facing, fold the quilted cuff together matching the raw ends.
9. Fold back the lining and batting and pin the top surface seams together.
10. Hand sew the top surface only using a ½″ (1.3 cm) seam allowance, keeping the lining and batting free.
11. Overlap the batting on the seam, and trim if necessary. Turn one side of the lining under and overlap it on the other side. Blind stitch it down. Turn the cuff right side out.

12. Insert the cuff inside the leg with the right side of the cuff toward the wrong side of the stocking. Match the raw edges around the top with the cuff seam matching the back seam of the leg.
13. Machine stitch using a ½″ (1.3 cm) seam allowance. This seam will be on the outside of the stocking but will be hidden by the cuff. Zigzag the edge of the seam to prevent ravelling if desired.
14. Pull out the cuff and turn it down over the top of the leg. Slip stitch lace or eyelette embroidery trim around the lower edge of the cuff on the under-side.
15. Make a hanger from wool to attach to the top of the stocking.

CHRISTMAS PATCHWORK WREATH (Plate 15)

This wreath makes use of another old favourite pattern — Dresden Plate. Each wedge represents one segment of the pattern. The completed wreath will have a diameter of 12″ (30.5 cm).

Materials Required

Twenty-eight wedges cut from a variety of calicos or Christmas fabrics
Twenty-eight wedges cut from lining fabric — this will not show
One piece of red broadcloth, measuring 7½″ x 35″ (19 cm x 89 cm), for the
  bow
Polyester fibrefill to stuff 28 wedges

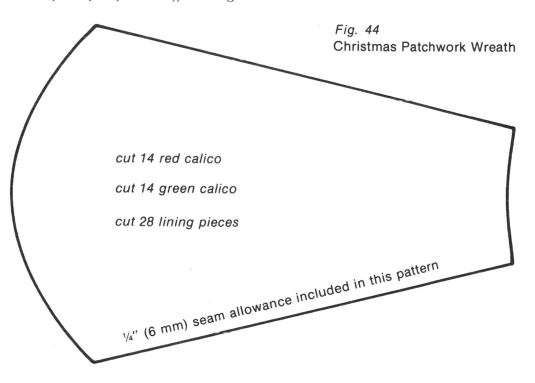

Fig. 44
Christmas Patchwork Wreath

cut 14 red calico

cut 14 green calico

cut 28 lining pieces

¼″ (6 mm) seam allowance included in this pattern

Sewing Instructions

Since the wreath will be machine sewn and the seam lines can be accurately gauged, the ¼″ (6 mm) seam allowance is included in this pattern for easier matching of the raw edges. Remember, in this pattern the pencil line will be your cutting line.

1. Trace the pattern on the wrong side of the material and cut the required number of red and green wedges remembering the pencil line is your cutting line. Cut out the lining wedges.
2. The wreath is made in two circles — the front and the back — which are then sewn together. Lay out two circles of 14 lining wedges each. Lay one calico wedge, right side up, on each piece of lining, alternating the red and green colours. Each calico wedge and its lining piece will be treated as a "unit" which will form a "pocket" to hold the polyester fibrefill.
3. With right sides of the calico facing, place two units together, matching the raw edges. You now have four layers of material — a lining wedge, a calico wedge topped with another calico wedge and another lining wedge.
4. Starting at the inner edge, machine sew ¼″ (6 mm) from the edge along the length of one side of the two units to within ¼″ (6 mm) of the outside edge. The seam allowance on the outer edge of the wreath needs to be free to allow the scallops to take proper shape when the wreath is turned right side out.
5. Open the two units and lay them out flat with their right sides up. Attach another unit to one of the sewn units and continue until the circle is complete.
6. Repeat for the second circle.
7. With right sides facing, place the two circles together and machine stitch using a ¼″ (6 mm) seam allowance around the inner edge.
8. Clip the curve almost to the seam line approximately twice in each wedge.
9. Turn the two circles right sides out with linings facing and stuff each one of the 28 pockets. Do not overstuff or it will be difficult to sew the outer edge together. The wreath should be firm enough to hang without loosing its shape. Work the fibrefill well down into the inner corners to make the wreath stand out firmly.
10. Turn and pin the scalloped edge of each circle treating the lining and the front as one piece so that the raw edges of the two circles are turned inside the wreath.
11. Baste and blind stitch the edges together. Work the fibrefill into the outside corners.

12. You are now ready to make the bow. With right sides facing, fold the red strip of broadcloth in half.
13. Machine stitch using a ¼″ (6 mm) seam allowance along the raw edges, sewing each end on the bias and leaving an opening for turning. Trim the points of the two ends, turn and press flat. Tie a bow and fasten it to the wreath.

CHRISTMAS COASTERS (Plate 15)
As well as protecting your furniture, these coasters in pretty Christmas fabrics make a colourful addition to a Christmas table when used under juice or water goblets on a plain red or green cloth.

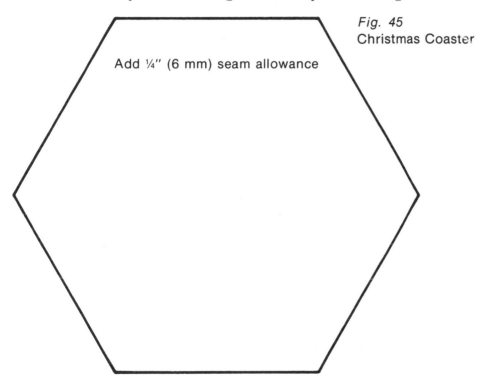

Fig. 45
Christmas Coaster

Add ¼″ (6 mm) seam allowance

Sewing Instructions
Make a template from the pattern and trace the pattern on the wrong side of the fabric, adding a ¼″ (6 mm) seam allowance when cutting. For each coaster you will need a red or green calico print for the front, a contrasting plain broadcloth for the back and a piece of quilt batting.

Lay one back and one front piece, right sides together, on top of the batting, making sure all points and raw edges are even. Sew on the seam line leaving a small space open on one side to turn the coaster right side out. Turn the coaster right side out. Blind stitch the opening closed. Be careful to pull out the corners. Press lightly and then quilt all around ¼″ (6 mm) from the outside edge.

APPLIQUÉD CHRISTMAS GUEST TOWELS   (Plate 15)
This is a pretty and inexpensive way to dress up your bathroom for Christmas or nice to give to someone as a gift. Any appliqué pattern may be substituted; use your imagination for finishing the ends.

Materials Required for Two Towels
One 39″ (1 m) length of 16″ (40.6 cm) wide huck towelling
Small pieces of calico and broadcloth for the appliqués
Embroidery thread if needed for embroidery
One strip of red broadcloth, measuring 3″ x 16″ (7.6 cm x 40.6 cm), to bind
  one end of the bell towel

Bell Towel With a Bound End
  1. Cut a 17″ (43.2 cm) long piece of towelling.
  2. Turn one end under ¼″ (6 mm) onto the back of the towel. Then turn down again, this time by ¾″ (1.9 cm). Pin, baste and hem to the towel.
  3. Press a ¼″ (6 mm) seam allowance on both long sides of the red strip of broadcloth. Fold it in half lengthwise with the pressed edges even. Bind the raw end of the towel with this, turning both ends in evenly.
  4. Make templates for the bell pieces from Fig. 47. Cut out the bell pieces allowing a ¼″ (6 mm) seam allowance. Use a print for the outside of the bell and a plain fabric for the oval lining piece of the inside of the bell at the bottom. Cut one clapper.
  5. Turn under the edges of the clapper and appliqué to the lining piece with one edge of the clapper touching the upper seam line in the middle of the oval lining.
  6. Turn the edge under and appliqué the lining piece to the front of the bell where indicated, placing the bottom edge of the lining oval on the seam line at the bottom of the bell.
  7. Turn under the edge of the bell all around.
  8. Centre it on the towel at a pleasing angle about ¾″ (1.9 cm) above the bound end of the towel and appliqué in place.
  9. Embroider two lines across the bell where indicated with three strands of thread.
  10. Trace on the pattern lines for the ribbon above the bell and embroider with three strands of embroidery thread. Press well.

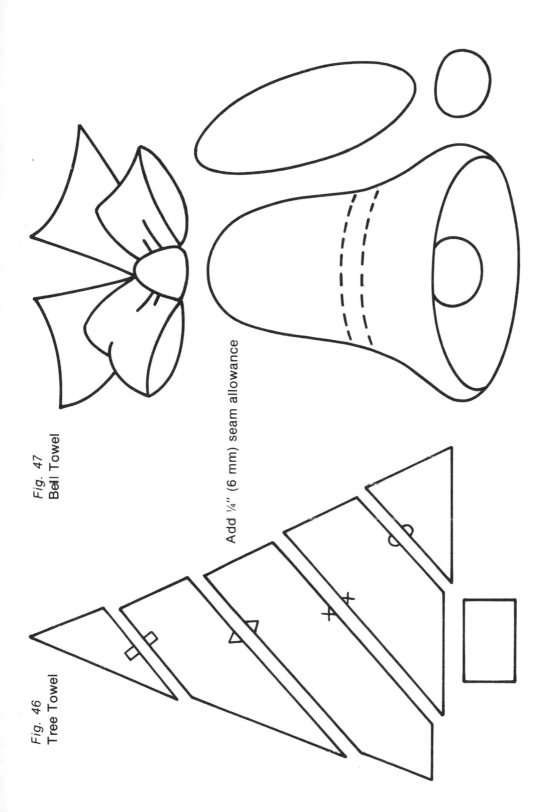

Fig. 47
Bell Towel

Add ¼" (6 mm) seam allowance

Fig. 46
Tree Towel

Christmas Tree Towel With Hemmed Ends

Cut a piece of towelling 18″ (45.7 cm) long. Both ends may be hemmed as directed for the bell towel. One end may be finished with an ornate embroidery stitch either by hand or on your machine.

1. Make templates for the Christmas tree pattern pieces as shown in Fig. 46.
2. Using different materials for each of the five strips, trace the patterns for the tree on the back of the material. Cut out, adding a ¼″ (6 mm) seam allowance. Make sure to mark on the symbols for matching the various strips. Cut one green trunk.
3. Sew the strips together to form the tree and centre the trunk at the bottom.
4. Clip the seam allowance at the corners of the trunk where it joins the tree.
5. Turn the edges under ¼″ (6 mm) and baste.
6. Centre and appliqué the tree to the towel about 1¼″ (3.2 cm) above the hem line. Press well.

CHRISTMAS PLACE-MATS   (Plate 15)

In this section I have given directions for an appliquéd mat and a reversible puff place-mat. Also try making up the Ohio Star pattern as directed in "Patchwork Place-Mats," p. 47, but using Christmas fabrics and colours. Hot mat covers may be made to match the place-mat set as directed in "Quilting Small Projects," p. 52.

CHRISTMAS PUFF PLACE-MAT   (Plate 15)

This is a reversible place-mat made from 15 rectangles, each one completed and then sewn together. The same method may be used to make a puff quilt although a quilt may need to be tied if the squares are very large.

Materials Required for One Place-Mat

Fifteen rectangles measuring 3 5/8″ x 4″ (9.2 cm x 10 cm) for each side of the mat — seven plain and eight calico. If you wish to make the mat reversible then choose your colour scheme for each side.
Fifteen rectangles of quilt batting the same size as the surface fabric

Sewing Instructions

1. Trace the required number of rectangles for each side of the mat on the material. Cut, allowing a ¼″ (6 mm) seam allowance on all sides.
2. Lay out the pieces for both sides of the mat on top of each other in the order in which they are to be sewn together.

3. With right sides facing, place the two pieces of fabric for one rectangle on a piece of batting.
4. Machine stitch on three sides. Trim the corners and turn right side out.
5. Blind stitch the fourth side. Press lightly.
6. Complete the remaining rectangles in the same fashion.
7. Lay out the completed rectangles in the order in which they will be sewn together.
8. With right sides facing, blind stitch the rectangles together in rows making sure that the shorter edges will form the top and bottom of the place-mat and the longer edges will form the ends.
9. Stitch the rows together. The place-mat is now complete and reversible.

CHRISTMAS WALL-HANGING (Plate 15)

This is a bright and cheery hanging for your home at Christmastime.

Materials Required

One piece of neutral coloured background material, measuring 16½″ x 21½″ (42 cm x 54.6 cm)
Two framing strips of red broadcloth, measuring 3½″ x 27½″ (8.9 cm x 69.9 cm) for the sides
Two framing strips of red broadcloth, measuring 3½″ x 22½″ (8.9 cm x 57.2 cm) for the ends
A small amount of red broadcloth for the ribbons
One piece of quilt batting, measuring 22½″ x 27½″ (57.2 cm x 69.9 cm) long
One piece of material for the backing, measuring 22½″ x 29″ (57.2 cm x 73.6 cm)
Three 7″ (17.7 cm) squares in contrasting calicos for the bells
Three pieces of contrasting broadcloth, measuring 2″ x 7″ (5 cm x 17.7 cm), for the bell liners
Three purchased pom-poms for the clappers
One 24″ (61 cm) long piece of wood dowling, ½″ (1.3 cm) in diameter
One 39″ (1 m) length of cording for hanging
Embroidery cotton

Sewing Instructions

The pattern pieces given for the bells and the bow are full size. The pattern for the ribbon at the bottom of the hanging must be enlarged to scale.

1. Trace all the pattern pieces on the right side of the various materials. Cut out and clip the curves if necessary.
2. Baste the raw edges on the ribbon and bow pieces under except

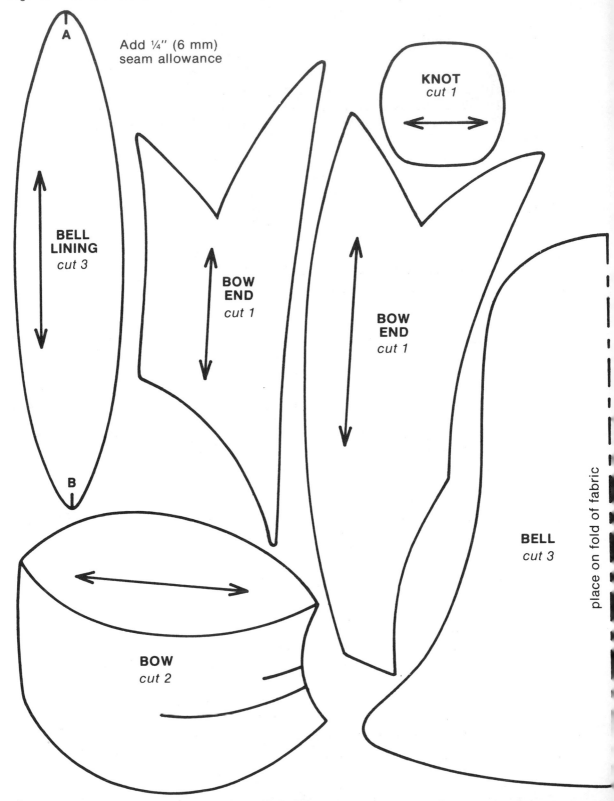

Fig. 48   CHRISTMAS WALL-HANGING

Add ¼" (6 mm)
seam allowance

A

**BELL
LINING**
cut 3

B

**BOW
END**
cut 1

**BOW
END**
cut 1

KNOT
cut 1

BELL
cut 3

place on fold of fabric

BOW
cut 2

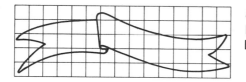

Fig. 49
Merry Christmas
Ribbon

1 square = 1" (2.5 cm)
Add ¼" (6 mm) seam allowance
cut 1

the ends of the ribbon which tuck under the bow pieces and the ends of the bows which fit under the centre knot.

3. Clip the seam allowance to the seam line on the bell lining piece at points A and B.
4. Turn under the seam allowance on the upper edge of the lining to these two points.
5. Appliqué the turned under top edge of the lining to the bell matching the sides and lower edge seams with bell seams.
6. Baste the outer edges together and treat as one unit.
7. Baste the seam allowance under all around each bell.
8. Turn under the edges on the "Merry Christmas" ribbon for the bottom of the hanging.
9. Arrange all the pieces on the background material, tucking under the ends of the bell ribbon as described above. Pin well. Baste in place and appliqué all pieces to the background.
10. Write "Merry Christmas" on a piece of paper in a size which will fit on the appliquéd ribbon. Trace this onto the ribbon using white dressmakers' carbon. Embroider through the ribbon and background material with three strands of embroidery cotton.
11. Sew the side and end framing strips on using ¼" (6 mm) seam allowances allowing the strips to overlap at each corner by 3¼" (8.2 cm). Mitre the corners. Press the front of the wall-hanging well and press the seam allowances toward the frame.
12. Mark on any necessary quilting lines, i.e., on the bell bow.
13. Press the top edge of the front of the hanging under ¼" (6 mm).
14. Lay the backing of the hanging, right side up, on top of the batting. Then lay the appliquéd front right side down on the backing piece. The backing piece will extend 1¾" (4.5 cm) above the top of the front piece and the batting. Follow the instructions as given in "Wall-Hangings," p. 64, for finishing your wall-hanging.
15. Finally, sew on the three pom-poms as clappers for the bells.

INDEX